1968: Art and Politics in Chicago

1968: Art and Politics
in Chicago

September 18 –
November 23, 2008

Copyright © 2008
DePaul University
Art Museum
Chicago, Illinois

ISBN-10
0-9789074-4-2
ISBN-13
978-0-9789074-2-6

Inside Cover Image:
Police move through
a haze of tear gas
in Lincoln Park. Photo
by Art Shay / Time &
Life / Getty Images

This exhibition is funded
in part by a grant from
the Terra Foundation for
American Art.

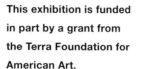

TERRA
FOUNDATION FOR AMERICAN ART

1968: Art and Politics in Chicago

DePaul University Art Museum

ACKNOWLEDGMENTS

In organizing this exhibition we have benefited enormously from the kindness and generosity of friends and colleagues in a variety of fields. We are grateful to the artists and their family members who have lent or facilitated the loan of their works: Donald Baum and Marie Baum, Hans Breder, Dominick Di Meo, Robert Donley, Ellen Lanyon, John Miller, Gladys Nilsson, Claes Oldenburg, Tom Palazzolo, Marc Paschke, Richard Paschke, and Sharon Paschke, Suellen Rocca, James Rosenquist, Peter Saul, Carol Summers, and William Weege; and to artists' representatives who have provided invaluable guidance: Carey Ascenzo, Oldenburg van Bruggen Studio; Beverly Coe, Charlotte Lee, James Rosenquist Inc.; and Shelley Lee, Roy Lichtenstein Foundation. Christo and Jeanne-Claude were a helpful source of information and encouragement.

Museums have lent generously to the project, and we thank James Cuno, Darrell Green, and Jackie Maman at the Art Institute of Chicago; Stephen Fleischman, Richard Axsom, Marilyn Sohi, and Carl Fuldner at the Madison Museum of Contemporary Art; Daniel Keegan and Stephanie Hansen at the Milwaukee Art Museum; Marla Price, Rick Floyd, and Allie Hughes at the Modern Art Museum, Fort Worth; Madeleine Grynsztejn, Lynne Warren, Amy Lukas, and Jennifer Draffen at the Museum of Contemporary Art, Chicago; George Davis and Jeremy Strick at the Museum of Contemporary Art, Los Angeles; Sylvia Rocciolo at the New School for Social Research; Anthony Hirschel, Angela Steinmetz, and Natasha Derrickson at the Smart Museum of Art; and Adam Weinberg, Barbi Spieler, Matt Heffernan and Berit Potter at the Whitney Museum of American Art. Private collectors have graciously agreed to important loans to the exhibition: Daniel Cohn, Chicago; Roy and Mary Cullen, Houston; Lew and Susan Manilow, Chicago; Betsy Rosenfield, Lake Forest, Illinois; and Irving Stenn, Chicago.

Art galleries have proved to be an important source for information and loans, and we owe a great debt to those who have enthusiastically assisted the project: Russell Bowman and Caelan Mys, Russell Bowman Art Advisory, Chicago; John Corbett and Jim Dempsey, Corbett vs. Dempsey, Chicago; Katherine Chan and Sarah Fritchey, David Nolan Gallery, New York; Melissa De Medeiros, Knoedler and Company, New York; Richard Feigen, Frances Beatty, and Susie Kantor, Richard L. Feigen & Company, New York; Richard Gray and Emily Ballard, Richard Gray Gallery, New York; Karen Lennox, Karen Lennox Gallery, Chicago.

Colleagues at libraries and other research institutions have located and provided access to specialized materials, and we acknowledge with gratitude their professional contributions: Scott Krafft, Nick Munagian, and Sigrid Perry, McCormick Library of Special Collections, Northwestern University; and Erin Tikovitsch, Chicago History Museum. We thank Abe Peck for information, and for sharing materials from his archive of the *Chicago Seed*. At DePaul University we have received much help from Paul Jaskot, Susan Solway, and Simone Zurawski of the History of Art and Architecture Department, and we particularly note the research contributions of Marie Elliott and Anne Wells, undergraduate art history students, and Blythe Sobol, recently graduated. The Museum staff has worked tirelessly on the exhibition; as registrar Laura Fatemi has handled complex loan, shipping, and installation issues with perfect finesse, and Christopher Mack, our assistant curator, has smoothly shaped both form and content in every aspect of the exhibition.

Interviews with those involved with the events of 1968 form an important part of this publication, and many thanks are due to the subjects and their interlocutors: Dominick Di Meo and Robert Cozzolino, Richard Gray and Christopher Mack, Ellen Lanyon and Joanna Gardner-Huggett, and Robert Sengstacke and Amor Kohli. Our guest curator Patricia Kelly, Assistant Professor in History of Art and Architecture and a scholar of contemporary art, initially proposed the idea for the exhibition, an outgrowth of her interest in Barnett Newman's still-shocking sculpture *Lace Curtain for Mayor Daley*. She has navigated the turbulent waters of recent local history with energy, openness, and keen perception, and we have all admired and learned from her spirit of inquiry. Her research has been generously supported by the DePaul Humanities Center.

Finally, we thank the Terra Foundation for American Art, and in particular Elizabeth Glassman, Elisabeth Smith, and Carrie Haslett. Without the extraordinary support and encouragement the Foundation offered the exhibition would quite simply have been impossible to achieve.

—**Louise Lincoln**, *Director*

FOREWORD

From the vantage point of forty years, the social and political climate of 1968 appears outsized, chaotic: a roiling period of dystopic and calamitous events domestically and internationally. There were aggressive military actions (the Tet Offensive, the Soviet invasion of Czechoslovakia); assassinations (Martin Luther King in April, Robert Kennedy in June, Fred Hampton in December); massive strikes in the capitals of Europe and on American campuses; the shocking atrocity of My Lai; a tainted American electoral process; and violent uprisings in cities around the world: Mexico City, Paris, and indeed in Chicago. The year 1968 is rightly understood as a moment of profound change in the civil rights movement, in public opinion about the Vietnam War, in gender and generational relations, change that echoed in every aspect of society. The fulcrum was the Democratic National Convention and its surrounding events: a week in August when the deep schisms in the country were manifested in chaos and violence in the streets of Chicago, and the reverberations were lasting.

This exhibition focuses on artists, in Chicago and elsewhere, who were catalyzed by those events and responded by participating in a series of high-profile exhibitions held around the city at the time of the 1968 elections. The present project does not attempt to recreate these shows, but rather to examine through them the larger question of whether artists, like writers, musicians, and other cultural workers, can participate effectively in social and political discourse through the medium of their work. And because no moment in time is entirely discrete and isolated, our study also encompasses objects from a prescient 1967 exhibition focused on Lyndon Baines Johnson, as well as material from a somewhat later Chicago exhibition on the general topic of violence. In the span between the *Portraits of LBJ*, whose satiric tone is well represented by Ellen Lanyon's puppet of Johnson, and the violence show, exemplified by Roy Lichtenstein's menacing *Pistol*, lay 1968.

Despite their importance in the moment many of the works have not been shown in the intervening years, and it has required patient research and sleuthing on the part of Patricia Kelly, our guest curator, to locate dispersed objects in private collections, in artists' own collections or estates, or some-times in the less-frequented areas of art dealers' storerooms. In many (although not all) cases, the works were distinct from the artists' oeuvres: they visually encode the passion and tragedy of the moment. Perhaps no piece better demonstrates this radical refocusing than Hans Breder's *Homage to Chicago 1968* sculpture: one of the pristine, polished Minimalist metal cubes he was making at that time, but this one ripped through by a gunshot. It is tempting to claim that the injection of politics into the art world around 1968 not only changed art, but had political effects as well. There may indeed be ways that this is true, but as Patricia Kelly argues in the following essay, the interrelation was complex and subtle, and the tensions and contradictions it produced are with us still. The art world, then and now, is not unitary, and we are fortunate to be able to include here the first-hand perspectives of four principal actors whose diverse vantage points enrich our understanding of that moment of collision between art and politics.

It is nearly impossible to avoid seeing the events of 1968 through the prism of 2008, noting the coincidence of a heated presidential election during an unpopular war, although there are manifold differences between the two eras. The larger issues—what are the social responsibilities of the individual? Do artists speak to a moment in time or to something timeless?—are constant and perhaps best understood not as questions than can be answered but rather as the focus of an ongoing, engaged, and high-stakes debate.

—Louise Lincoln, *Director*

Sept. 5 1968

Dear Dick and Lottie,

The deadline has come and gone on this ad and the
reason I have nothing as yet is that the events in
Chicago threw me into a confusion. In Chicago, I,
like so many others, ran head-on into the model
American police state. I was tossed to the ground
by six swearing troopers who kicked me and choked
me and called me a Communist. Fortunately my head
wasnt split, my wrists broken, or my groin gored,
but I got the message - the evil in Chicago (which
is considerable) had been mobilized to destroy the
values I came looking for. I was trying to do the
city a favor, but the sore-covered cur would have
none of it. Which is why I am confused: a gentle
one-man show about pleasure seems a bit obscene in
the present context. Evil unsettles me, it doesnt
inactivate me, but if evil is the subject, a show
about Chicago requires rethinking. Can you postpone
my show?

                              Claes

*(letter from Claes Oldenburg to the dealer Richard Feigen postponing a scheduled one-man show;
Feigen Gallery's "Richard J. Daley" was its replacement.)*

PATRICIA KELLY

ART AND POLITICS, CHICAGO-STYLE: 1968

8

For one week in August 1968, the Democratic National Convention (DNC) turned Chicago into a war zone, pitting government forces against anti-Vietnam War protesters in a mass-media showdown, and effectively polarizing the American public into pro- and antiwar camps. On the side of authority was Richard J. Daley, the Democratic mayor of Chicago and an autocratic leader who had vowed to maintain stability in his city at any cost (fig. 1). Committed to keeping the convention in Chicago, Daley gave no ground to protesters, denying public permits for marches and demonstrations and calling in reinforcements from the U.S. Army and the Illinois National Guard.[1]

Figure 1. Mayor Richard J. Daley at the International Amphitheater, August 28, 1968. AP Images.

In the weeks leading up to the convention, the city prepared for battle, even surrounding the site of the convention, the International Amphitheater, with barbed wire. It appeared Daley intended to make good on his promise: "[a]s long as I am mayor of this city, there will be law and order on the streets."[2]

Conversely, the dissenters were disparate in both ideology and strategy. They represented various antiwar organizations, including Students for a Democratic Society (SDS), the National Mobilization Committee to End the War in Vietnam (Mobe), and the Youth International Party (Yippies), known for their highly theatrical, antiestablishment actions (fig. 2).[3] Though early predictions estimated over 100,000 demonstrators would descend on Chicago, in reality, due to fears about the potential violence and growing alienation among political activists, only about 10,000 people showed up.[4] Despite such reduced numbers, the DNC quickly devolved into chaos, both on the convention floor and in the streets. These events demonstrate the deep social anxieties and divides permeating this historical moment, and they were mediated not just in relation to direct political engagement, but also on the cultural front.

The clash between Daley's forces and the protesters began immediately, with the violence intensifying as the convention wore on: on Sunday, August 25, the eve of the convention, police began nightly raids on Lincoln Park to prohibit protesters from camping out; the next day activists were repeatedly dispersed by police as they marched from Lincoln Park through Old Town on their way downtown; and on Tuesday additional National Guard troops were brought into the city to quell the escalating hostility and augment the Chicago police (fig. 3).[5] One of the worst confrontations took place the following evening in front of the headquarters of the Democratic Party, the Conrad Hilton Hotel at the corner of Michigan and Balbo Avenues (fig. 4). As protesters hurled rocks, bottles, and expletives, the police fought back with Mace, clubs, and even motorcycles, used by some patrolmen to run down people in the street. As Don Sullivan, a reporter for *Chicago's American* who was reporting live back to the news desk, described it, "The cops are clubbing everything in sight. God…they don't care who they slug. Girls. Kids…anything that moves. There are 250 sitting in the intersection of Michigan and Balbo. Police are wading in. I can hear screams" (fig. 5).[6] One of the groups particularly targeted by police was the press. As reporters and photographers bore witness to the events, the cops turned on the media.[7] Cameras were broken, film confiscated, and heads were clubbed. Chicago was in the middle of what was later termed "a police riot," and with approximately 600 citizens arrested, the meaning of freedom in a supposedly democratic state was drawn into question (fig. 6).[8]

The chaos at the convention, broadcast on the nightly news, was for many a tipping point in what had already been a long and difficult year. On April 4 Martin Luther King was assassinated, instigating riots in major U.S. cities including Chicago, and on June 5 Robert Kennedy, an antiwar candidate, was killed after winning the California primary. When it became clear that Vice President Hubert Humphrey, a proponent of President Johnson's war policy, would be the Democratic nominee, many antiwar protesters felt the election itself was meaningless. A sense of doomed inevitability contributed to what were already well-established feelings of disenfranchisement, particularly among the younger generation. As Abbie Hoffman and Jerry Rubin of the Yippies advised, the best way to deal with a fraught political sphere was to reject its foundational principles: "Nobody goes to work. Nobody goes to school. Nobody votes. Everyone becomes a life actor of the street doing his thing, making the revolution by freeing himself and fucking up the system."[9] In short, freedom could only be gained by actively rejecting traditional values, a perspective fundamentally in conflict with Daley's vision of Chicago.

2.

3.

4.

Figure 2. Yippie marchers during the Democratic National Convention. Photo by Julian Wasser/Time & Life Pictures/Getty Images; **Figure 3.** Police move through a haze of tear gas in Lincoln Park. Photo by Art Shay/Time & Life/Getty Images; **Figure 4.** National Guard unit at the Conrad Hilton Hotel, August 28, 1968. © Bettmann/CORBIS.

The most polemical group involved in the protests was undoubtedly the Yippies, and much of the city's wrath was directed against them. Using media exposure to heighten their political aims, the Yippies for months prior to the convention had been advertising what they called "an invasion of Chicago," complete with demonstrations, street fairs, free public concerts and performances. The plan was to stage "a festival of life" beginning with the nomination of a pig for president (fig. 7).[10] The Yippies wrote articles, published fliers, and held rallies to announce their plans for Chicago, circulating farcical rumors: Yippies would pick up delegates at the airport and drive them to Wisconsin, "hyperpotent" male Yippies would be used to seduce delegate's wives, LSD would be dumped in the city's water supply, and the amphitheater would be stormed.[11] Their tactics played on the paranoia of the city's conservative constituents to incite fear, misunderstanding and a sense of impending doom. Hoffman acknowledged this as a strategy of obfuscation in his anarchist treatise *Revolution for the Hell of It*, written the same year as the convention: "Clarity, alas, is not one of our goals. Confusion is mightier than the sword."[12] Taking their cue from radical activist organizations such as the Living Theatre and the Bread and Puppet Theater, the Yippies practiced a form of guerilla performance reliant on spontaneity, improvisation, satire, and farce. Such emphasis on play and personal political engagement proved directly at odds with Chicago politics. The Yippies were speaking a language Mayor Daley could not understand.[13]

While the 1968 DNC further galvanized the antiwar movement both on a national and local level, protest was not new to Chicago. A vibrant antiwar community included a history of artist-sponsored activism beginning as early as 1966 (fig. 8). Artists with work as figuratively diverse as Dominick Di Meo, Robert Donley, Donald Main, and Jim Falconer founded the Chicago branch of Artists Against the War in Vietnam, with Di Meo's Kinzie Street apartment serving as the group's meeting place, production studio, and storage facility (fig. 9).[14] The Chicago art scene, to a large degree, mirrored what was happening in other major American cities: artists banding together to create collaborative protest actions and monuments. In New York City the Artists and Writers Protest "End Your Silence" campaign,[15] a petition signed by 579 visual artists, writers, musicians, and actors condemning American intervention in Vietnam, was printed in *The New York Times* in 1965, and Angry Arts Week was staged as a week-long program of antiwar events in 1967; while in Los Angeles in 1966 the Artist's Tower of Protest, a steel structure approximately 60 feet tall, was constructed and covered with over 400 panels produced by artists from across the United States.[16] But what makes the Chicago context unique is its almost total disappearance from the historical record. In fact, Chicago's art history has largely escaped programmatic scrutiny, and the history of artist-sponsored activism in the city even more so.[17] And while this exhibition will contribute to the literature, the larger, more comprehensive history of late 1960s cultural activism in Chicago has yet to be written.

The New York School painter Barnett Newman was among the first artists to respond to the Chicago convention riots. On September 3, he wrote to Charles Cunningham, Director of the Art Institute of Chicago, asking for the removal of his work from an upcoming exhibition on Dada and Surrealist art. Newman declared: "I do not want to be represented in this exhibition in protest against the uncalled-for police brutality of Mayor Daley, which fills me with disgust. I cannot in good conscience do otherwise."[18] A few days later, on September 5, Jesse Reichek, a professor of painting at Berkeley, and the New York artist Hedda Sterne proposed a two-year art boycott of the city, until 1970 when Daley's term as mayor expired. Supported by over 50 artists and reported in the *New York Times*, the

5.

6.

7.

13

Figure 5. Police and demonstrators near the Conrad Hilton Hotel, August 28, 1968. Photo by Les Sintay, © Bettmann/CORBIS; **Figure 6.** Michigan Avenue and Balbo Drive, August 28, 1968. © Bettmann/CORBIS; **Figure 7.** Yippies with Pigasus, the pig they nominated for president, August 23, 1968. © Bettmann/CORBIS.

14

8.

9.

Figure 8. Artists participating in antiwar demonstration, date unknown. Photo courtesy Dominick Di Meo; Figure 9. Artists participating in antiwar demonstration, date unknown. Photo courtesy Dominick Di Meo.

boycott statement read: "The recent actions by Chicago police, directed and supported by Mayor Daley and not repudiated by the people of Chicago, have marked that city as being unfit for membership in a civilized society. As painters and sculptors we know that art cannot exist where repression and brutality are tolerated."[19] The same day the boycott was announced the sculptor Claes Oldenburg, who was at the convention and caught up in the violence, sent a letter to the Chicago art dealer Richard Feigen canceling a one-man show at Feigen's gallery scheduled to open October 23, a show ironically intended to showcase the city in a positive light: "In Chicago, I, like so many others ran head-on into the model American police state. I was tossed to the ground by six swearing troopers who kicked me and choked me and called me a Communist…a gentle one-man show about pleasure seems a bit obscene in the present context" (see above, p. 7).[20]

To avert the negative impact such a boycott would have on Chicago museums and galleries, Feigen alternatively proposed the "Richard J. Daley" protest show, an exhibition intended to demonstrate the outrage of many left-leaning artists.[21] A manifesto was circulated with Feigen's proposal which artists (participating or not) were asked to sign. Addressing the global implications of the events in Chicago, Feigen's text states: "the week of Aug. 25 exposed the new class struggle. It is no longer the poor class against the rich or Democrat against Republican. It is the educated against the uneducated, the courageous against the terrified, young against old, thinking against nonthinking."[22] Many of the artists who originally agreed to the boycott shifted allegiance to participate in Feigen's show.[23] The Minimal sculptor Robert Morris still refused to exhibit, though he did send a telegram to Feigen on opening night advising, "Redo the Fire of 1871."[24]

The "Richard J. Daley" show provided an outlet for artists to both engage in a form of art activism and negotiate the role of art in relation to social crisis, while simultaneously staging a spectacle that drew national media attention.[25] Some artists, such as Sam Francis, Donald Judd, Kenneth Noland and Robert Motherwell, chose to present work in their conventional styles, eschewing any sort of direct political commentary. Motherwell, though socially committed with a long history of activism in liberal causes, was adamant about figuratively separating his politics from his art. Speaking about his contribution to the protest exhibition, an abstract expressionist painting (cat. no. 16), he explained: "There is a certain kind of art which I belong to. It can no more make a direct political comment than chamber music can. But by exhibiting with these artists who can, and with the theme of the exhibit, we are showing our support."[26] Others were more direct in their political statements, producing new work parodying the image of Mayor Daley himself. The pop artist James Rosenquist, for example, used an effigy of Daley's head in the poster for the exhibition, *See-Saw Class System* (cat. no. 30), which echoed the "new class struggle" evoked in Feigen's manifesto. Rosenquist also contributed *Portrait of Mayor Daley* (cat. no. 29), a screenprint reproduction of Daley's head in pink and white plastic, cut into ribbon-like strips. The work was intended to be interactive as the mayor's floating head could be physically distorted by the viewer's fist.

Even more contemptuous in tone, though similarly referencing the mayor's body, Newman's *Lace Curtain for Mayor Daley* (cat. no. 18), a six-foot by four-foot barbed wire sculpture framed in steel and splattered with red paint,[27] was positioned in the middle of the gallery, calling up the barriers attached to the front of government vehicles used as a means of crowd control (fig. 10).[28] The red paint splattered over the center reinforces this allusion, evoking a tangible trace of a physical body caught up against the jagged wire. Newman's title is no less provocative, parodying Daley's virile, authoritative power by linking it to the perceived femininity of lace. Using Daley's own Irish ethnicity as leverage, and in no small part as a response to the mayor's crass, anti-Semitic heckling of Connecticut Senator Abraham Ribicoff on the convention floor,[29] Newman pejoratively associated the mayor with the "lace curtain Irish," a well-recognized term in Chicago's working-class neighborhoods from which the mayor hailed.[30] To be labeled "lace curtain Irish" was to be seen as using material goods to mask one's working-class origins, attempting to mask an unrefined nature capable of the violence evident on the streets of Chicago behind the more delicate trappings of lace.[31]

Other works represented in the show include Red Grooms's four-foot-tall sculpture *Miss Napalm*, dressed in an American flag and bearing a striking resemblance to the Statue of Liberty; Christo's *Do Not Opened*, a wrapped package resembling a bundle of dynamite sticks (inadvertently destroyed); Hans Breder's polished aluminum cube shot through with a rifle (cat. no. 3); and Lee Bontecou's painted metal relief with a skeletal mouth (fig. 11). Oldenburg contributed two drawings for a colossal monument for the city of Chicago representing Daley's head on a platter (cat. no. 22, fig. 12), as well as 50-mini fireplugs (cat. no. 24), meant to mimic the city's distinctive hydrants (fig.13).[32]

The show was eclectic, exciting, and visually overwhelming. With artists working in a variety of representational and abstract styles, and no clear consensus on how to best register dissent, the reviews of the show were mixed. For example, Grace Glueck wrote in the *New York Times* that "by and large, the show goes in for the quick journalistic jab, relying heavily on boyish scatology, name-calling, and sight gags to make its protest points." Glueck's assessment underscores the larger dilemma facing artists interested in using their work as a direct means of ideological engagement: how to maintain artistic integrity, or avoid the trap of pure propaganda, while openly addressing acute political needs.

The "Richard J. Daley" show was not the first time a local art gallery had taken on the persona of a major political figure. Predating Feigen's exhibition by more than a year was "Portraits of LBJ" at the Richard Gray Gallery, which opened in February 1967.[34] The show was conceived as a retort to a controversy in the popular press regarding an official state portrait of President Johnson painted by the New Mexico artist Peter Hurd (fig. 14). From the onset of the commission Hurd was denied access to the president: he was only allowed two sittings with Johnson, during one of which the president was rumored to have fallen asleep. When the painting was unveiled in late 1966, Johnson rejected the portrait, describing it as "the ugliest thing I ever saw."[35] Clearly, after three years in the White House, Johnson was sensitive to how he was being represented, a concern that would only intensify as the war escalated. To left-leaning artists and intellectuals Johnson, like Daley, became a personification of political corruption, a hawk committed to a policy of Communist containment ensuring America's continued involvement in Vietnam.

As a means to solve the president's "image crisis," not just confined to portraiture, Gray organized an alternative show of proposed likenesses, with twenty-seven artists participating, most from Chicago.[36] While not all of the work on view was satirical, the majority lampooned Johnson by overemphasizing his particular physiognomy (especially exaggerating his nose and ears) and parodying his Texan background.[37] For example, Ellen Lanyon's *LBJ Doll* (cat. no. 13) is an approximately three-foot tall string toy depicting the president in cowboy hat and boots. With a smoking pistol in one hand and an American flag in the other, the doll was intended to be manipulated by the viewer, who could pull the strings to raise the president's arms and legs up and down. In Suellen Rocca's portrait, the *State of LBJ* (cat. no. 28) a contour map of Texas is filled in with guns, cowboy hats, cacti, and oil wells. Symbols of Johnson's complicated identity—president, cowboy, international media

10.

12.

11.

13.

Figure 10. Jeeps and barricades during the Democratic National Convention. ICHi-19630, Chicago History Museum, photographer unknown; **Figure 11. Lee Bontecou** (b. 1931), *Untitled*, 1965, welded and painted steel, soot. Des Moines Art Center's Louise Noun Collection of Art by Women through Bequest, 2003.269. Photo courtesy Des Moines Art Center; **Figure 12. Claes Oldenburg** (b. 1929), *Study for a Colossal Monument to Mayor Daley #1*, 1968, Photo courtesy the Oldenburg van Bruggen Foundation; **Figure 13. Claes Oldenburg** (b. 1929), *Fireplugs*, installation view of Richard Feigen Gallery, 1969. Photo courtesy the Oldenburg van Bruggen Foundation. Photo by Jonas Dovydenas.

14.

15.

Figure 14. Peter Hurd (1904–1984), *Lyndon Baines Johnson*, 1967, tempera on wood. National Portrait Gallery, Smithsonian Institution; gift of the artist. Photo courtesy National Portrait Gallery, Washington D.C.; Figure 15. Bill Mauldin (1921–2003), Poster for Chicago Response exhibitions, November 1968. Photo courtesy McCormick Library of Special Collections, Northwestern University, Evanston, Illinois.

figure, and ranch hand—mix with doodle drawings of ears, noses and other body parts. The very body of the president is reduced to such base constituent elements, signaling money, violence, and power. Even more direct in tone, Seymour Rosofsky's *End of the Trail* represents a pot-bellied native in full regalia bearing a striking resemblance to Johnson.[38] Seated on top of a tired horse at the rim of a canyon, the rider appears both comical and tragic, perhaps calling up Johnson's own politically precarious position.

This harsh view of Johnson was mirrored in the polls: by May 1967, a Harris survey indicated a nearly two-to-one negative rating for the president, with the majority of Democrats and previous Johnson supporters giving him poor reviews.[39] In response to an invitation by Gray to attend the opening of "Portraits of LBJ," Johnson's assistant cordially wrote: "The President is appreciative of your invitation," but because of his many other commitments could not attend.[40]

Gray's show, while less serious than Feigen's exhibition, provides a model of sorts for "Richard J. Daley" by centering on an individual political figure, demonized by the left. One major difference, however, was the real political stake involved in taking on Daley, particularly at a time when he was fighting to justify police agression during the convention week. As Feigen acknowledged: "Mayor Daley reigned supreme, dictator of all that lay within the vast city limits," even "all the powerful Republicans—the old Chicago families who lived in Lake Forest and on the Near North Side, the money that really owned the town...supported Daley." Daley's supporters threatened to close down the Feigen exhibition, angered by the extensive press coverage of the show. The gallery was trashed and Feigen, who had already moved to New York City to run a second gallery, hired a bodyguard to protect his staff.[42] Moreover, Feigen's allegiance to many New York artists meant his show was populated with fewer local artists. The "Richard J. Daley" exhibition was, ironically, more

national in scope, providing a venue where artists who did not witness the events could register their response, but it also reinforced a historical divide between New York and Chicago, which did not advance the work of local artists.

Following Feigen's lead, ten other Chicago galleries, most no longer extant, followed suit.[43] On November 2, 1968, the weekend before the national election, these galleries banded together for a one-day special event "Response to Violence in our Society," with Bill Mauldin designing the poster for the event, a flower emerging from behind barbed wire (fig. 15).[44] The proceeds from admission fees and a portion of all sales were donated to the American Civil Liberties Union, which had undertaken the defense of those arrested during the convention (see below, p. 26).[45] There was also a special invitational "Response" exhibition held in the lobby of Robert Snyder and Associates, a design studio near the gallery district.[46] With 60 Chicago artists participating, this show, like the "Richard J. Daley" exhibition, was intended to break the proposed boycott, and also to galvanize the local arts community towards some sort of effective political action.[47] In a letter soliciting participation, the organizers explained their intentions by quoting at length from Hilton Kramer's condemnation of the boycott as published on September 22 in the *New York Times*: "It is reasonably certain that Mayor Daley will not suffer the loss of a single night's sleep over this selective boycott. The only losers are sure to be the very people who abhor what Mr. Daley represents. If the boycott is effective, Chicago's art institutions and art community will be thoroughly demoralized...and the forces of reaction will have gained an unanticipated dividend on their violence."[48]

Collectively reviewed as "angry but brilliant" in the Chicago press, the Response shows were celebrated as a particularly local reaction to the violence at the convention, and for many seemed more viscerally engaged than the Feigen exhibit. As Robb Baker argued in the Chicago Tribune: "One difference in basic concept spelled success for the 'Response' show. Instead of limiting themselves, as Feigen did, to 'name' artists—most of whom had not been in Chicago during the Democratic Convention and thus had only secondhand feelings about what occurred—the 'Response' galleries opened their doors to practically anyone who had what they felt was a valid reaction...."[49] Here, almost inadvertently, Baker acknowledged the competitive tension that existed between New York and Chicago artists, especially as many well-known "second city" artists like Claes Oldenburg and Red Grooms had relocated to New York, and Chicago collectors, dealers such as Feigen, and cultural institutions often favored New York artists.[50]

The fierce political engagement of these exhibitions and the speed with which they came together serves as testament to the pressing social crisis.[51] Yet the urge to respond in some sort of creative capacity to the immediacy of the moment stood in sharp contrast to the depoliticized legacy of modern art.[52] From the late 1940s onwards, formalist modernism, as championed by Clement Greenberg, seemingly distanced the art object from political engagement, separating aesthetic debates from everyday concerns.[53] As questions regarding the future of painting and the implications of new media took center stage, many artists also began actively debating how art could intercede in social issues. The personal was increasingly recognized as the political.[54] In what was an emergent postmodern moment, individual subjectivity and identity became fertile sites for creative experimentation.

With a diverse collection of work exhibited at these various shows, some directly responding to Mayor Daley and others that represented the "signature styles" of participating artists, the protest shows collectively demonstrated how the realities of late-1960s politics came crashing into the fine-art establishment, forcing many politically ambivalent artists, regardless of individual style, to active participation. While little documentation exists of the Response shows, possibly because of their short duration, the work of the exhibiting artists represented a wide array of media, from the prints of the German Expressionist Käthe Kollwitz to the experimental films of local artists John Heinz and Tom Palazzolo (cat. no. 25), both connected to the activism circulating around Dominick Di Meo's Chicago studio.

At the Richard Gray Gallery, the politically charged prints of William Weege were on view. Known for his collaged popular—culture references—Hollywood film stills, racy images of women, newspaper photographs of politicians, and anatomical illustrations[55]—Weege, like many in the Feigen show, directly satirized Mayor Daley. For example, in his *Richard is a Wise Ole Owl* (cat. no. 41), the head of the owl is cut out, leaving a void in the shape of the Chicago police shield. Inside this "frame," Daley's head is perched on the owl's body, caught in mid-sentence and looking slyly out at the viewer. The Philip Freed Gallery of Fine Art showcased a portfolio produced as an antiwar benefit by the organization Artists and Writers Protest Against the War in Vietnam, also known as Artists Protest. The group, which started in 1965, took part in antiwar marches, and in 1967 sponsored Angry Arts Week. Its intention was to "make our protest not through rallies or marches but through work in our own fields," but not necessarily work that was explicitly political.[56] For example, in a boxed edition prints by artists Rudolf Baranik, Carol Summers (cat. no. 33), Mark di Suvero (cat. no. 6), Leon Golub, Louise Nevelson (cat. no. 17), Ad Reinhardt (cat. no. 27), and others, were auctioned off with a folder of poems by various writers including Robert Creeley, Robert Duncan, Denise Levertov, Joel Oppenheimer, and James Wright.

The pervasive inquiry dominant throughout the Response shows into issues of war, brutality, power, and aggression was taken up by another exhibition held that same fall at the Museum of Contemporary

Art in Chicago. A few days after Richard Nixon's presidential victory in November, an exhibition planned well before the convention riots, "Violence in Recent American Art" opened, gathering together a diverse body of largely representational work.[57] Examining five different types of violence—war, racial, personal, gun-related, and psychological—this exhibition took conflict, more broadly defined than the events in Chicago, as its subject matter responding to what was seen as an increase in brutality and aggression. Curator Robert Glauber explained:

> Over the past year or so, Americans have taken to a serious discussion of violence… the constant barrage of bloody news from the battlefronts in Vietnam, the shocking murders of Martin Luther King and Robert Kennedy, the persistence of riot and death on our streets, the physical brutality often employed to counter protest…all of these have helped crystallize the conscience of a nation.[58]

The cover of the exhibition catalogue underscores Glauber's point. Designed to mimic the front page of a tabloid newspaper, yet reporting actual news events from the past few years, the headlines juxtapose violent episodes and public apathy across the United States: "Mother of 7 Found Guilty in Torture Slaying of Girl," "3 Policemen Cuffed Together and Killed," and "37 Who Saw Murder Didn't Call the Police." The show fit within what was a larger debate in the U.S. about the efficacy of violence as a strategy for political change, particularly as deployed among some antiwar groups, the U.S. military, and the Black Power Movement.[59] But this debate also resonated globally as the student uprisings in Paris in May, the Prague Spring in Czechoslovakia, and numerous other protest and liberation movements of 1968 used violence as a primary tool.

Further, this supercharged context led many cultural and political theorists to examine the subject. For example, Hannah Arendt's *On Violence* was a specific response to what she viewed as a misplaced "faith in violence" as a means to achieve freedom from oppressive power structures.[60] She argued that violence is not an effective solution for legitimizing conflict as the implements of violence were now so technically and scientifically advanced that their destructive potential could never justify the potential political goal. Here she directly opposed the perspective of the French existentialist thinker Jean-Paul Sartre, who viewed "revolutionary violence" as a way to reclaim power from the "systematic violence"[61] enacted by colonial rule. In fact, Sartre was one of the first intellectuals to throw his support behind the French student protesters and their use of subversive and violent tactics, just as he had for the Algerian rebels a few years before.

It is this larger discourse regarding violence and its societal implications that the MCA exhibition addressed. Representing a range of artists from across the U.S., the violence show included an eclectic array of subjects and media. Images that sexualized violence, such as Bernard Aptekar's *A Death Dealer* and William Weege's *Fuck the C.I.A.* (cat. no. 37), were juxtaposed with work that addressed the gravity of race relations and abuses of power, including Andy Warhol's *Race Riot* (cat. no. 34). Yet most of the work was less specific, focusing on general questions of power, authority, and violence in everyday life. This prevailing interest by 1960s artists in social interrelations and lived experience paralleled a simultaneous inquiry on the part of the New Left into subjectivity and issues of identity. Looking to incipient post-structuralist theories developing in the writings of Herbert Marcuse, Henri Lefebvre, Louis Althusser, and others, many factions of the New Left were examining how power operates both on and through the individual.[62] The goal for artists and activists alike was free self-expression, personal autonomy, and committed social action, all means to combat the alienation of contemporary social life.[63]

A reconsideration of the events of 1968, forty years later and during another presidential election year with the United States again a nation at war, allows for the exploration of some of the larger questions at play both then and now regarding the relationship between politics and art: How does art redefine itself in response to ideological conflict? Can culture productively intervene in and illuminate crises in the broader society? And more pointedly, what are the social responsibilities of the artist in a time of war? In the late 1960s and early 1970s, these questions were part of an overarching inquiry on the part of the art establishment into the terms of political and aesthetic engagement, a discourse that obligated many artists and critics to address the political, even if only to dismiss its importance to contemporary art. Thus, while it was still possible in 1967 for Philip Leider, the editor of *Artforum*, the preeminent art journal of the day, to argue "I prefer to live as if there were no connection between the two enterprises, politics and art,"[64] by 1970 even Leider, who was committed to the legacy of formalist modernism, had to recognize the pressures of the political by allowing space in the magazine for a regular column on politics and art. "I was dragged by the times, kicking and screaming, but I just felt it had to happen.... I didn't want anything to do with politics, I didn't want it in the magazine. But I knew that I had to make an opening for it."[65]

Yet while many in the art establishment were pushed towards increased political activism, questioning systems of authority and institutions of power, there was no clear consensus on how to proceed. This was the first time the art world was politicized since the 1930s; the leftist movement was basically disbanded during the Cold War.[66] One of the only New York artists who remained a committed socialist during these years, Ad Reinhardt provided younger artists with one model of political engagement, but even he was conflicted. While promoting the social responsibility of the artist in 1962, Reinhardt rejected politicization of the art object: "Art is art-as-art and everything else is everything else."[67] By 1966, however, Reinhardt produced an antiwar painting for the Los Angeles Tower of Protest,[68] though he later denounced this sort of protest art: "I think an artist should participate in any protests against war—as a human being. There's no way they can participate as an artist without being almost fraudulent or self-mocking .... There are no effective paintings or objects that one can make against the war."[69] Reinhardt's contribution to the Artists Protest Portfolio (cat. no. 27) in 1967 seems to reinforce this position. Not a traditional work of art, but a postcard covered in text, Reinhardt's piece is addressed to the "War Chief." On its face, the artist lists declarative statements such as "No War, No Imperialism, No Murder, No Napalm," while on the back he implicates the art establishment: "No Art of War, No Art in War, No Art to War, No Art on War..."

Such confusion over exactly how to respond to political crisis continued throughout the late 1960s, a consequence of increasing activism among artists and galvanizing events like the 1968 DNC. This culminated in a symposium organized by *Artforum* during the summer of 1970 on the issue of the artist and politics.[70]

Responding in part to the recent killing of four Kent State students by National Guardsmen in January of that same year, the symposium expressed the ideologically diverse opinions of its twelve contributors,[71] from the complete disavowal of the mixing of art and politics by the painter Walter Darby Bannard: "Political things should not affect the *making* of art because political activity and art-making have never mixed to art's advantage,"[72] to Irving Petlin's call for increased political activism among artists: "I will join with people into any direct political action that strikes back at this layered and spaced brutality called the 'administration.'"[73] The Minimal sculptor Donald Judd, caught between a belief in activism by artists and in an art for art's sake, argued both for wholesale political involvement and the complete segregation of the art object from the realm of politics.[74] For Judd, artists should act first and foremost as citizens, on a regional and local level, and use

16.

17.

18.

19.

Figure 16. Protesters holding skulls designed by Miriam Brofsky, date unknown. Photo courtesy Dominick Di Meo; **Figure 17.** Protesters with artists' banner, date unknown. Photo by Bernard Beckman and Tom Palazzolo. Photo courtesy Tom Palazzolo; **Figure 18. Dominick Di Meo** (b. 1927), *Landscape Beautification Johnson Style,* date unknown, Photomechanical print. Courtesy of the artist; **Figure 19.** Police at the International Amphitheater, site of the Democratic National Convention, August 26, 1968. © Bettmann/CORBIS.

artworks for overt political purposes only "when nothing else can be done."[75] His insistence that in relation to social issues "art may change things a little but not much," was indicative of his belief that politics, like art, exists in its own sphere of activity, governed by its own rules and systems. For Judd, the only way to intervene in political problems, therefore, was to address them head on and in their own terms.[76] Here, Judd's position aligns with that put forth by the Frankfurt School theorist Theodor Adorno in his essay "Commitment" (1962), where he insisted that an art true to its own logic, an art for art's sake, was in itself sociopolitical in nature.[77]

While the *Artforum* symposium was composed of artists living in New York, the debates raised regarding social responsibility and individual engagement were transferable to the Chicago context, as local artists were similarly struggling with how best to address mounting political concerns. The activities of Artists Against the War in Vietnam provided one haven for like-minded artists, though the work of individual members was stylistically diverse and incorporated a range of media.[78] Dominick Di Meo, for example, was at the time creating both reliefs of skulls, bones, and appendages out of plastic and papier-mâché as well as collage paintings, but these did not overtly reference current events. Distinct from his personal work, Di Meo contributed to the agitprop being produced in his studio space used for the group's protest marches— the LBJ butcher apron, the styrofoam skulls designed by Miriam Brofsky, and the artist's protest banner (figs. 16 and 17). Additionally, though done separately from the group, Di Meo printed *Landscape Beautification Johnson Style*, which he handed out in front of the Art Institute of Chicago to radicalize students and promote the antiwar movement (fig. 18). Robert Donley, on the other hand, allowed politics to more directly influence his art production, particularly in his *Waiting* (cat. no. 7). Composed of soldiers and helicopters on a fiery ground, his work was exhibited in a group show of mainly Chicago artists sponsored by Mobe and held at the Chicago Coliseum during the DNC.[79]

Regardless of the multiple ways art is affected by such turmoil, organizations like Artists Against the War in Vietnam provided an important outlet to relieve some of the building societal pressure on artists, and to rethink the possibilities of aesthetic engagement outside of formalist Modernism. And Chicago was an important site in which to work this through, particularly because of its investment in figuration. The Monster Roster of the 1950s, producing existential, semi-mystical work, and the Hairy Who, which had come to prominence through a series of exhibitions at the Hyde Park Art Center beginning in 1966, secured the city's imagist reputation and a distinction from the colorfield painting prominent in New York.[80] Such difference provided a certain freedom (the flip side of disadvantage) to artists working in Chicago, who due in part to the sporadic nature of institutional support were proactive in establishing alternative art spaces and initiating other professional opportunities.[81] One precursor to the activism of the late 1960s was Exhibition Momentum, an art show originally set up to protest the exclusionary submission practices of the Art Institute of Chicago's annual exhibitions of Chicago artists, which prohibited students from submitting work.[82] Such artist-oriented mobilization for political change laid the groundwork for the political organization of the late 1960s, providing a framework of opposition and methodical protest.

With this in mind, the brutality evidenced at the 1968 Democratic National Convention, and its inherent irony— that a meeting of the more liberal political party in the U.S. could make a mockery of individual freedom and the right to dissent—had widespread societal implications for the cultural establishment, specifically in Chicago (fig. 19). The various Response exhibitions, and the resulting dialogue on the relationship between politics and art, are a case in point. Until now, this history has largely remained unwritten, focused instead on the proposed boycott initiated in New York, and Feigen's "Richard J. Daley" show comprised of predominantly national artists. In order to understand the complexities of this moment, this history needs to be linked back to the specificities of site, and the political realities of the late 1960s Chicago art scene.

The last exhibition to address the fallout from the 1968 DNC was Oldenburg's solo show held at Feigen's gallery in the spring of 1969. In a sense, this is an appropriate end point, as by 1970 artist-sponsored political activism turned increasingly inward, no longer focusing on Vietnam but rather on artists' rights and institutional critique.[83] Within this context, Oldenburg's Chicago exhibition in hindsight functions as both an indictment of political power and a reification of a particular painful moment in the city's history, an acknowledgment of trauma and the beginning of catharsis. The show, which had been planned for the previous fall, started in 1967 as a celebration of Oldenburg's "home" city. But over the course of the next two years, it morphed into a much less positive view of Chicago, preoccupied with the presence of Mayor Daley and the convention itself.[84] Through a series of what Oldenburg termed constructions, models, and drawings, the artist proposed a set of monuments for the city, some feasible and others visionary, that would demonstrate the inherent contradictions of Chicago's political and social landscape using humor and satire as primary tools.

A recurrent element in the show was the iconic Chicago fireplug, originally designed by the Chicago Water Works in 1916, which Oldenburg had already exploited in a series of multiples for the Feigen protest show (cat. no. 24). Explaining his fascination with the fireplug, Oldenburg singled out its anthropomorphic characteristics that could easily "represent the body of either sex."[85] Referencing the DNC, Oldenburg further explained: "The Fireplug (Chicago Style) became the receptacle for most of my reports from the site, a subject which "by supreme coincidence, means everything—

an inventory of nature in all its states, including opposites."[86] So, for example, in *Study for a Soft Fireplug, Inverted* (cat. no. 23), the fireplug appears vulnerable, slumped over and battered like the bodies of protesters (or Oldenburg's own body) during the convention riots, while in *Proposal for a Skyscraper in the Form of a Chicago Fireplug* (cat. no. 20) the hydrant becomes the inverse, a gigantic phallus towering over the downtown landscape in a bold display of patriarchal power. But not all the work in the show images the fireplugs or overtly references the convention. *Notebook Page: Smoke Studies During the Burning of Chicago* (cat. no. 21) focuses instead on the chaos that broke out after the assassination of Martin Luther King in April, foreshadowing the DNC violence by referencing the looting, arson, and rioting that occurred on Chicago's West Side, a crisis that prompted Mayor Daley to issue his infamous "shoot to kill" order.

Oldenburg used culture to work through the spectacle of real-life political events, both on a personal level and writ large through the pervasiveness of mass media. For Oldenburg, as for the rest of the artists included in these Chicago protest exhibitions, the crux was to find some way to negotiate a rapidly shifting social dynamic in which the modernist rules of artistic engagement that insulated the art object were no longer in play. As these shows demonstrate, there was no one strategy (abstract or figurative) that worked for all of the exhibiting artists, but a multitude of positions and perspectives on art's potential in a time of war. While there is more work to be done when examining the late 1960s Chicago art scene, this study provides a framework for rethinking how art connected with politics at a particularly fraught historical moment. As the events of the 1968 Democratic National Convention remind us, the meaning of art is continually shifting depending on societal needs. With the current war in Iraq now in its fifth year, another systemic inquiry into the possibilities of art to refocus political discourse is long overdue.

PARTICIPATING GALLERIES / EXHIBITIONS

Richard Gray Gallery
620 North Michigan

-William Weege-
Dramatic silk-screen and photo off-set images which reflect this
artist's personal response to violence.

Kovler Gallery
952 North Michigan

-Enrico Sarsini-
A Life-photographer's photographs of the Washington Freedom
March, 1964

Lo Guidice Gallery
157 East Ontario

A funny thing happened on my way to the Convention – Poetry, Still
Photography and Film dealing with the events of Convention week
in Chicago

Pro-Grafica Art Gallery
155 East Ontario

Anti-war statements; 17th century to the present – Bauermeister,
Beckmann, Callot, Goya, Groz, and Lawrence Shahn.

Rosner's Student Gallery
235 East Ontario

A Juried show of the best student work from all the schools dealing
with protest and violence.

Distelheim Gallery
113 East Oak Street

-Richard Beard-
The artist portrays the human condition of Man.

Faulkner Gallery
646 North Michigan

-Kathe Kollevitz-
Whose life-time preoccupation was with social protest and
anti-violence.

Philip Freed Gallery of Fine Art
920 North Michigan

Artists and writers protest against the War in Vietnam.
A portfolio of 16 artists icluding Golub, Nevelson, and Sugarman.

Allan Frumkin Gallery
620 North Michigan

Films by John Heinz and Tom Palazzolo: Of Protest and
the Democratic Convention 1968

Galleria Roma
155 East Ontario

Interpretations of protest and violence.

SPECIAL CHICAGO ARTISTS' SHOW – RESPONSE
601 North Fairbanks Court

(Response exhibitions list, October 1968. Document courtesy Ellen Lanyon)

1   Frank Kusch, *Battleground Chicago: The Police and the 1968 Democratic National Convention* (Chicago: University of Chicago Press, 2008), 51-3. Daley doubled the strength of the Chicago police force, bringing in 5,000 army troops and an additional 5,000 members of the Illinois National Guard. Paul Potter of the Students for a Democratic Society (SDS) described the city as "an armed camp… we just couldn't quite get it through our heads that all of that force was being lined up against us." See Terry Anderson, *The Movement and the Sixties: Protest in America from Greensboro to Wounded Knee* (Oxford: Oxford University Press, 1995), 217.

2   Mayor Daley in a speech before the American Legion in July 1968, as quoted in J. Anthony Lukas, "Dissenters Focusing on Chicago," The *New York Times* (August 18, 1968), 64.

3   Mobe was an umbrella organization that included many antiwar collectives, providing a general framework for mass demonstrations and coordinating efforts between individual groups.

4   Anderson, 215-20. As Anderson acknowledges, many protest groups were divided over whether to participate: "SDS headquarters in Chicago announced that it was not interested in demonstrating with liberals… The Chicago Area Draft Resisters stated they were 'too individual' to participate in mass mobilizations. Except for a few veterans of the Poor People's Campaign, most blacks showed little interest in what they called 'White man's politics.' Other activists disliked the Yippies, some seeing them as apolitical, irrational, freaks, while others viewed them as provocative radical New Yorkers on an ego trip."

5   For a description of the various altercations between police and protesters see Kusch, 70-93.

6   *Chicago's American* (August 29, 1968), 1, 3. Reprinted in Kusch, 105.

7   Kusch, 75-8.

8   A national inquiry chaired by Chicago Crime Commission director Daniel Walker, reporting to the National Commission on the Causes and Prevention of Violence set up by Lyndon B. Johnson in 1968, described the confrontations as a "police riot." See Daniel Walker, *Rights in Conflict* (New York: Bantam Books, 1968).

9   Jerry Rubin and Abbie Hoffman, "Yippie Manifesto" (1968), *"Takin' It to the Streets" A Sixties Reader*, eds. Alexander Bloom and Wini Breines (New York and London: Oxford University Press, 1995), 323.

10 See David Farber, *Chicago '68* (Chicago and London: The University of Chicago Press, 1988), 3-28; and Anderson, 217-19.

11 For more on Yippie tactics see David Lewis Stein, *Living the Revolution: The Yippies in Chicago* (New York: Bobbs-Merrill, 1969).

12 Abbie Hoffman, *Revolution for the Hell of It* (Cambridge, Mass.: Da Capo Press, 2005), 26.

13 One of the most publicized Yippie events occurred on August 24, 1967, when Hoffman and other Yippies entered the New York Stock Exchange and dropped dollar bills on the trading floor causing pandemonium and a disruption in trading.

14 Robert Cozzolino, "Where have you been all my life, *Dominick Di Meo?*," *Dominick Di Meo: The Man in the Moon–Paintings, Drawings, and Reliefs, 1947-75* (Chicago: Corbett vs. Dempsey, 2008), 4-5.

15 "End Your Silence," The *New York Times*, June 27, 1965. After likening US involvement in Vietnam to French colonialist practices, the signatories affirmed: "American artists wish once more to have faith in the United States of America. We will not remain silent in the face of our country's shame." This statement was signed by over 500 writers and artists, including Norman Mailer, Elaine de Kooning, Ad Reinhardt, Harold Rosenberg, and Mark Rothko.

16 Angry Arts Week included a film series, an artist's collage, a children's festival, and a traveling caravan of actors, poets, and musicians. For more on the antiwar activism of US artists in the late 1960s see Francis Frascina, *Art, Politics and Dissent: Aspects of the Art Left in Sixties America* (Manchester: Manchester University Press, 1999).

17 Kevin Consey notes this lack of art historical scholarship on Chicago in his foreword to the Museum of Contemporary Art's exhibition catalogue *Art in Chicago 1945-95* (New York and London: Thames and Hudson, 1996), 8. There are no truly comprehensive historical studies of Chicago art available. Some studies that look at specific aspects of Chicago's art past include: John Corbett and Jim Dempsey, *Big Picture: A New View of Painting in Chicago* (Chicago: Chicago History Museum, 2007); Robert Cozzolino, *Art in Chicago: Resisting Regionalism, Transforming Modernism* (Philadelphia, PA: Pennsylvania Academy of the Fine Arts, 2007); Franz Schulze, *Fantastic Images: Chicago Art Since 1945* (Chicago: Follett Publishing Company, 1972); and Dennis Adrian, *Chicago Imagism: A 25 Year Survey* (Davenport, IA: Davenport Museum of Art, 1994).

18 Reprinted in *Barnett Newman: Selected Writings and Interviews*, 43.

19 See Dan Sullivan, "Artists Agree on Boycott of Chicago Showings," The *New York Times* (September 5, 1968). This statement alludes to fact that many Chicagoans, both before and after the convention, supported the Mayor and his policies. A week prior to the convention, an editorial in the *Sun-Times* praised Daley for setting up tough "ground rules" to ensure order and eliminate "irresponsible activities." On the Sunday after the convention a group of citizens staged a demonstration in the city to thank the police for all their efforts. See Kusch, 55 and 114.

20 Letter from Oldenburg to Richard Feigen dated September 5, 1968. The letter was later used as promotional material for Feigen's "Richard J. Daley" exhibition. Reprinted in "Artists vs. Mayor Daley," *Newsweek* (November 4, 1968), 117.

21 The Richard J. Daley protest show ran from October 23 to November 23, 1968. In an interview with Staci Boris in 1996, Feigen described a conversation he had with one of the artists organizing the boycott: "I called these people. I can't remember which artist, one of those crotchety old biddies that was running around having nothing better to do, and I said, 'Who are you hurting? Do you think Daley cares if the artists exhibit their work? All you're doing is hurting your comrades here, they're the ones who are going to notice and suffer. Boycotting them— a terrible idea. Make a statement, not a non-statement.' So I started or ganizing quickly, to counteract this…" Archives, Museum of Contemporary Art, Chicago.

22 Reprinted in D. J. R. Bruckner, "The Art World Answers Chicago's Mayor Daley," *Los Angeles Times*, Calendar Section (October 20, 1968), 59.

23 Donald Janson, "Anti-Daley Art Put in Show in Chicago," The *New York Times* (October 24, 1968). The artists included in the original Feigen show were Robert Barnes, Jack Beal, Lee Bontecou, Hans Breder, Enrique Castro-Cid, Christo, George Cohen, William Copley, Ed Flood, Sam Francis, Leon Golub, Adolph Gottlieb, Red Grooms, Henry Hanson, Charles Hinman, Hans Hollein, Ray Johnson, Allen Jones, Donald Judd, Donald Kaufman, Nicholas Krushenick, Gerald Laing, Stanley Landesman, Roy Lichtenstein, Richard Lindner, James McGarrell, Charles Mingus III, Robert Motherwell, Lowell Nesbitt, Barnett Newman, Kenneth Noland, Claes Oldenburg, Irving Petlin, Bernard Pfriem, Robert Rauschenberg, Hans Richter, Larry Rivers,

James Rosenquist, Seymour Rosofsky, Peter Saul, Alfons Schilling, Aaron Siskind, Richard Smith, Tony Smith, Harry Soviak, Theodoros Stamos, Frank Stella, Chuck Thomas, Jean Tinguely, Jack Tworkov, John Willenbacher, and Derrick Woodham.

24 Somewhat ironically, the telegram itself was put on view as a work of art, both in the original Feigen show and in the 20th anniversary show Feigen staged in 1988.

25 The New York Times estimated that 10,000 people visited the show in Chicago, before it traveled to the Contemporary Arts Center in Cinncinati, where it opened on December 20, 1968. A reduced version of the show, which included 40 works, also made a brief stop at Feigen's Greene Street gallery in New York in February 1969. Grace Glueck, "40 Art Works Inspired by the Mayor of Chicago," The New York Times (February 22, 1969), 23.

26 "Artists vs. Mayor Daley," Newsweek (November 4, 1968), 117.

27 Ann Temkin, ed., Barnett Newman (New Haven and London: Yale University Press, 2002), 298. As the eyebolts on the top suggest, Lace Curtain for Mayor Daley may have been intended as a hanging piece, and in fact Don Lippincott, whose company fabricated the work, remembers the artist suspended the piece at the plant. This, of course, fits with the curtain reference of the title. However, when the piece was shown at the Feigen Gallery, it was supported on cinder blocks, possibly because of concerns over its weight. Since then, the work has always been displayed standing.

28 Daniel Schulman in a letter to Armin Zweite, dated November 22, 1996. Barnett Newman, Lace Curtain for Mayor Daley, Object File 1989.4333, Art Institute of Chicago.

29 Daley could be seen broadcast to approximately 8 million television viewers emphatically yelling at Ribicoff. While the sound was cut by the networks, the words were easily discernible by reading lips: "Fuck you, you Jew son of a bitch. You lousy motherfucker, go home." See David Burner, Making Peace with the 60s (Princeton, NJ: Princeton University Press, 1996), p. 213. To this blatant display of anti-Semitism by Mayor Daley, Newman responded, "Well if that's the level he wants to fight at, I'll fight dirty-too; there're other words besides 'kike.'" Hess, p. 123.

30 Daley grew up in the ethnically white neighborhood of Bridgeport, a historically Irish American neighborhood that was birthplace to a half-dozen of Chicago's most prominent mayors.

31 If the lace curtain references domestic middle-class values and the sanctity of the bourgeois home, Newman connects this with the bloody confrontations of the public sphere in Chicago. The domestic lace curtain, transformed into barbed wire, stands in for the most famous of curtains in post-WWII American political rhetoric: an iron one, more gentrified, perhaps, but with equally repressive tendencies securely in place.

32 Oldenburg produced 100 of the fireplugs, but only 50 were shown in the gallery.

33 Glueck, 23.

34 "Portraits of LBJ" was on view at Gray's gallery from February 6 through February 11, 1967. It was then exhibited at the Chicago Cliff Dwellers Club, on Michigan Avenue on top of Symphony Hall, for the month of March, 1967.

35 "The President: Another Image Problem," Newsweek (January 16, 1967), 22. Apparently Johnson favored a portrait done by Norman Rockwell, which he showed to Hurd in a scene that Lady Bird Johnson later described as so inflamed, she hoped never to experience another like it, "even if she lived to be 100."

36 The artists who participated in the show include: Don Baum, Miriam Brofsky, Dominick Di Meo, Stanley Edwards, Jim Falconer, Maurice Fouks, Roland Ginzel, Jack Harris, Peter Holbrook, George Kokines, Ellen Lanyon, June Leaf, Mary McCarty, Gladys Nilsson, Jerry Pinsler, Kerig Pope, Bob Post, Jack Powell, Ray Reshoft, Suellen Rocca, Seymour Rosofsky, Roy Schnackenberg, Alice Shaddle, Irene Siegel, Tom Simpson, Sherry Vilas, and Karl Wirsum.

37 According to one reviewer, at least three of the exhibited works portrayed Johnson in a more flattering light: Roy Schnackenberg's "Johnson" depicts the president in respectful attention in front of a coffin-like box, Jack Powell's "Astronaut's Funeral" portrays the president weeping, and "LBJ" by Sherry Vilas is a noncommittal pop image.

38 Here, Rosofsky references a work of the same name by the sculptor James Earle Fraser. Produced in 1915 for the Panama-Pacific Interna tional Exposition in San Francisco, this sculpture depicts a Native American slumped over on an emaciated horse. The spirit of dejection evident in the piece symbolized the idea that native people had been pushed to the edge of extinction, a common belief in the early twentieth century used to marginalize native peoples from political debates.

39 This is not surprising as by 1967 the expanding Vietnam War oversha-dowed domestic affairs, particularly Johnson's "Great Society," a package of social reforms intended to eliminate domestic poverty and racial injustice. As the war intensified, Johnson announced on March 31, 1968 he would not seek reelection, fearing his fall in the polls would cost him a second term. Bruce Altschuler, "Lyndon Johnson and the Public Polls," The Public Opinion Quarterly 50 (Autumn 1986), 288.

40 On January 27, 1967, W. Marvin Watson as Special Assistant to the President, after receiving an invitation to the opening, sent a letter stating Johnson's regrets: "I regret that because of the many commitments he already has, it will be impossible for the President to be with you. Please accept our best wishes and our appreciation for your thoughtfulness in writing." Archives, Richard Gray Gallery, Chicago.

41 Richard Feigen, Tales from the Art Crypt (New York: Alfred A. Knopf, 2000), 235.

42 Richard Feigen, catalogue essay, "Richard J. Daley," The 20th Anniversary, October 1988.

43 The Response shows included Distelheim Gallery, "Richard Beard Paintings;" Faulkner Gallery, "Käthe Kollwitz;" Philip Freed Gallery of Fine Art, "Portfolio–Artists' and Writers' Protest;" Allan Frumkin Gallery, "Films by John Heinz and Tom Palazzolo;" Galleria Roma, "Law and Disorder and Graffiti;" Kovler Gallery, "Enrico Sarsini;" Lo Guidice Gallery, "A Funny Thing Happened on My Way to the Convention;" Pro Grafica Art, "From the 17th Century to the Present;" Rosner Student Gallery, "Special Response Exhibit;" and Richard Gray Gallery, "William Weege."

44 Six women formed the organizing committee for the Response shows: Phyllis Kind, Muriel Newman, "Bumpy" Rogers, Sally Shorey, Nora Smith, and Sally Wardwell.

45 General admission tickets were $2.50, students could gain entry for $1, and children under 12 were admitted free.

46 Whitney Halstead, "Chicago," Artforum (January 1969), 64-5.

47 According to a checklist for the exhibition, the artists participating in the show included: Franz Altschuler, Vincent Arcilesi, Ralph Arnold, Don Baum, Vera Berdich, Fred Berger, Alvydas Biciunas, Vladimir Bubalo, Virgil Burnett, Cosmo Campoli, John Cannon, Dominick Di Meo, Robert Donley, Elizabeth Eddy, Ruth Esserman, James Falconer, Lillian Desow

28

Fishbein, Edward Flood, Maurice Fouks, Jose Garcia, Roland Ginzel, Art Green, George Griffin, Theodore Halkin, Kathleen Hart, Peter Holbrook, Michael Hurson, Miyoko Ito, Richard Jeske, Vaughn Kurtz, Paul Lamantia, Ellen Lanyon, George Longfish, Allan Lunak, Ben Mahmoud, Don Main, Edward Majeski, Mary McCarty, Douglas McGarvey, Robert Middaugh, Ruth Migdal, John Miller, Ed Pashke, Don Pellet, Al Pounian, Rodney Quircioni, Bern Rauch, Charles Reynolds, Seymour Rosofsky, Richard Sessions, Alice Shaddle, David Sharp, Irene Siegel, Karen Stern, Volkerding de Bolanos, Jerome Walker, Karl Wirsum, Pricilla H. Witek, John Weber, and Ray Yoshida. Ellen Lanyon, personal archives.

48   Letter of solicitation for the invitational Response show. Ellen Lanyon, personal archives.

49   Ross Baker, "'Response' show, is current, tough," *Chicago Tribune*, Section 1A (November 3, 1968), 8.

50   Cozzolino, *Art in Chicago: Resisting Regionalism, Transforming Modernism*, 9. Cozzolino cites Franz Schulze, *Fantastic Images: Chicago Art Since 1945*, 7, 37; originally written in 1972. He also recounts a conversation between Schulze and the artist Theodore Halkin on a perceived indifference to Chicago artists on the part of local collectors, critics, and art institutions. See Schulze, 30-1.

51   Some of the shows, such as the Weege exhibit at the Richard Gray Gallery, were scheduled before the convention.

52   Baker, 8. Some of the galleries kept the work on view for longer period: the Weege show at the Richard Gray Gallery closed sometime in December, the Rosner exhibit was on view through December 7, the Pro Graphica show was on view until the end of September, and Galleria Roma and Lo Guidice kept their shows up just a few additional days.

53   For Greenberg, in the best of modernist painting, flatness, shape and color were of primary importance; while representational imagery or literary or historical narrative was superfluous as it deflected attention from pictorial effects. Greenberg attempted to underscore the critical nature of formalism and its grounding in a Kantian enlightenment model in his article "Modernist Painting." See Clement Greenberg, "Modernist Painting (1960)," *Clement Greenberg: The Collected Essays and Criticism*, vol. 4, ed. John O'Brian (Chicago: University of Chicago Press, 1993), 85-93.

54   Carol Hanisch coined this phrase in her essay of the same name originally published in *Notes From the Second Year: Women's Liberation*, Shulamith Firestone and Ann Koedt, eds. (New York: Radical Feminism, 1970). For an artist's interpretation of the phrase, see Martha Rosler, " Well, is the Personal Political?" (1980), *Feminism–Art–Theory: An Anthology 1968-2000*, ed. Hilary Robinson (Oxford: Blackwell, 2001), 95-6.

55   "Peace Is Patriotic" is a series of 25 collage prints Weege produced as his M.F.A. thesis at the University of Wisconsin, Madison. Nearly half of the prints satirize President Johnson, and many of the prints were used as posters to advertise different antiwar events. The print "Fuck the C.I.A." was included in the "Violence" show at the MCA. See Robert Epp, "Bill Weege: Peace is Patriotic," Gallery One One One, University of Manitoba. March 15-30, 2007.

56   Julie Ault, *Alternative Art New York: 1965-1985* (Minneapolis: University of Minnesota Press, 2002), 17-8.

57   Participating artists included Bernard Aptekar, Ralph Arnold, John Balsley, Warrington Colescott, William Copley, Dominick Di Meo, Jim Dine, Roslyn Drexler, Douglas Edge, Stanley Edwards, Ed Flood, Peter Holbrook, Robert Indiana, Ray Johnson, Edward Kienholz, Paul La Mantia, Ellen Lanyon, Roy Lichtenstein, Ben Mahmoud, Robert Mallary, Richard Merkin, Robert Andrew Parker, Ed Paschke, Clayton Pinkerton, Albert Pounian, Joseph Raffael, Robert Rauschenberg, Peter Saul, Arthur Secunda, James Strombotne, Carol Summers, Andy Warhol, William Weege, William T. Wiley, and James Wine.

58   Robert Glauber, *Violence in Recent American Art*, exhibition catalog (Chicago: Museum of Contemporary Art, 1968), n.p. The exhibition was on view from November 8, 1968 through January 12, 1969.

59   Ironically, while the exhibition was in the planning stages, President Lyndon Johnson initiated his own inquiry into the roots of increased aggression, the National Commission on the Causes and Prevention of Violence (1968-9) chaired by Milton Eisenhower.

60   Hannah Arendt, *On Violence* (New York: Harcourt, Brace, & World, 1969).

61   Jean-Paul Sartre, *Colonialism and Neocolonialism* (New York: Routledge, 1964, 2006).

62   See, for example, Herbert Marcuse, *An Essay on Liberation* (Boston: Beacon Press, 1969), Henri Lefebvre, *The Critique of Everyday Life* (London and New York: Verso, 1947,1991), and Louis Althusser "Contradiction and Overdetermination," *The New Left Reader*, Carl Oglesby, ed. (New York: Grove Press, Inc, 1969).

63   Howard Brick, "Authenticity and Artifice," *Age of Contradiction: American Thought and Culture in the 1960s* (New York: Twayne Publishers, 1998), 66-97.

64   Philip Leider in a letter to Sidney Tillum dated September 30, 1967, Amy Newman, 14. Leider continued: "I know very well what it is like, however, to live as if there were not, and there the edge of discrimination turns not against the politics, but against the art."

65   Leider, as quoted in Newman, 264-5. The "Politics" column, which ran five times beginning in November 1970, was designated for "political communications from various segments of the art community."

66   As art historian Annette Cox has argued, activism among artists in the 1930s, much of which centered around the Communist-affiliated Artists Union, became increasingly difficult by the end of the decade. The revelations of Stalinist policies through the Moscow trials of 1936-8 and the signing of the Nazi-Soviet pact in 1939 disintegrated the artistic left in the U.S., leading to what was after World War II a strident anti-Communist fervor, with no room for criticism of the American political system or a discussion of the relationship between politics and art. See Annette Cox, *Art-as-Politics: The Abstract Expressionist Avant-Garde and Society* (Ann Arbor, MI: UMI Research Press, 1982).

67   Ad Reinhardt, "Art as Art," *Art International* VI (December 1962), reprinted in *Art in Theory 1900-1990: An Anthology of Changing Ideas*, eds. Charles Harrison and Paul Wood (Oxford: Blackwell Publishers, 1992), 806-9.

68   Frascina 81-2.

69   Reinhardt in a radio interview with Jeanne Seigel, broadcast June 13, 1967 on WBAI in New York City as part of a series entitled "Great Artists in America Today." This was reprinted in Seigel's *Artwords: Discourse on the 60s and 70s* (Ann Arbor, MI: UMI Research Press, 1985), 28.

70   "The Artists and Politics: A Symposium," *Artforum* (September 1970), 35-9. Other examples of the politicization of the art press include Dore Ashton, "Response to Crisis in American Art," *Art in America* 57 (January 1969), 24-35; and Gregory Battcock, "Marcuse and Anti-Art," *Arts Magazine* 43, no. 8 (Summer 1969), 17-9.

71   The twelve artists *Artforum* chose for publication were Carl Andre, Jo Baer, Walter Darby Bannard, Billy Al Bengston, Rosemarie Castoro,

Rafael Ferrer, Donald Judd, Irving Petlin, Edward Ruscha, Richard Serra, Robert Smithson, and Lawrence Weiner; all were invested in non-representational production to varying degrees.

[72] Walter Darby Bannard, "The Artist and Politics: A Symposium," 36.

[73] Irving Petlin, "The Artist and Politics: A Symposium," 38.

[74] Considering the issue of artist-organized activism, Judd specifically critiqued the Art Workers Coalitions and their targeting of the institutional policies of the Museum of Modern Art. Believing there was nothing intrinsically corrupt about institutions, especially one as "indifferent" as an art museum, Judd asked: "Why is the Modern so interesting? Why be so eager to demonstrate (against it), to use a tactic that was originally used for a much more serious purpose?" See Donald Judd, "The Artist and Politics: A Symposium," 37.

[75] Ibid.

[76] On Judd's political activism, particularly his affiliation with the War Resister's League and the Lower Manhattan Township, see David Raskin, "Specific Opposition: Judd's Art and Politics," *Art History* 24.5 (November 2001), 687-96.

[77] Adorno, paralleling claims made by Greenberg in his early essays, insisted that the intellectual rigor of modern art must be maintained in order to reserve a place for critical contemplation, as overtly political art can, within both totalitarian and capitalist societies, too easily be reduced to propaganda, manipulating its viewer towards certain ideological aims. See Theodor Adorno, "Commitment," *Notes on Literature, II*, trans. Shierry Weber Nicholsen (New York: Columbia University Press, 1991), 76-94.

[78] Core founding members of the group, also known as Chicago Artists for Peace in Vietnam, included Dominick Di Meo, Robert Donley, Tom Brand, Jim Falconer, and Donald Main, though the membership shifted to include a host of others: Miriam Brofsky, Dennis Kowalski, Tom Palazzolo, Charles Reynolds, and Jim Zanzi, to name just a few.

[79] Dominick Di Meo, telephone interview, July 24, 2008. About two weeks prior to the convention, Di Meo received a call from Mobe asking if he could put together a show of local artists to run in conjunction with the convention.

[80] The title "Monster Roster" was coined by Franz Schulze in 1959 to refer to the work of artists such as Don Baum, Dominick Di Meo, Leon Golub, June Leaf, and H.C. Westermann, among others. The Hairy Who included James Falconer, Art Green, Gladys Nilsson, Jim Nutt, Suellen Rocca, and Karl Wirsum. Dennis Adrian, et al., *Who Chicago?: An Exhibition of Contemporary Imagists* (Sunderland: Sunderland Art Gallery, 1980).

[81] Cozzolino, *Art in Chicago*, 9. See also Lynne Warren, *Alternative Spaces: A History in Chicago* (Chicago: Museum of Contemporary Art, 1984).

[82] Ibid., 11-12. See also Lynne Warren et al., *Art in Chicago 1945-1995* (London and New York: Thames and Hudson, 1996), 144.

[83] The Art Worker's Coalition, which was formed in January 1969, and the critical practice of the conceptualists Hans Haacke and Daniel Buren fit within this context. See Julia Bryan-Wilson, "Hard Hats and Art Strikes: Robert Morris in 1970," *Art Bulletin* 89 (June, 2007), 333-359.

[84] Claes Oldenburg and his family moved to Chicago from Stockholm in 1936. Twenty years later, in 1956, Oldenburg moved to New York City.

[85] *Claes Oldenburg: Constructions, Models, and Drawings*, exhibition catalogue (Chicago: Richard Feigen Gallery, April 30– May 31, 1969), section V.

[86] Ibid., section III.

Interviews

DOMINICK DI MEO | *interviewed by Robert Cozzolino*

Robert Cozzolino: Dominick, you were heavily involved in the antiwar movement in Chicago during the 1960s as an organizer and artist. I'd like to talk to you about your experiences protesting the Vietnam War and recollections of the events surrounding the 1968 Democratic National Convention. When did you first become involved in antiwar activities? I think you told me that you started getting involved in things as early as 1964?

Dominick Di Meo: Actually it was earlier but not in Chicago. When I was still in Italy, Kennedy was increasing advisors in Vietnam and I stood in front of the American consulate in Florence holding sign in English that said, "hands off Vietnam."

RC: What happened when you returned to Chicago?

DD: When I came back in 1964, there were demonstrations. The earliest I remember was either late spring or early winter at the Water Tower. It was a mild day but snow had fallen—the sun was out but there was slush everywhere, everything was melting. There were only thirty of us in the demonstration. It was led by a young Presbyterian minister and there were two artists involved: myself and Don Main. The police forced us to take a circuitous route where there was no activity like industrial areas and by the Congress Street expressway. We were passing a Navy recruiting station and we were attacked by the Navy personnel who made ice balls out of the slush and pelted us —they were hard as rock. Then another recruit put a stop to it, said that we had a right to demonstrate. While the ones who had attacked us went back into the station, he stayed out and he smiled at us, and I thought that if guys in the service were sympathetic, or at least not hostile, then the war wouldn't go too far. Little did I realize it would take twelve years before the war ended!

RC: Gradually you began making prints, posters, propaganda, right?

DD: It was a loose thing, mainly Don Main, Tom Brand and I. I had a two-floor loft on Kinzie Street near downtown, just by the river, kitty-corner to Marina Towers. I had a studio on one floor that became the epicenter for making silkscreens, papier-maché skulls [fig. 16], and other projects like the Artist's Banner. The Banner was painted there in my loft. We invited different artists do two-by-two-foot panels, antiwar messages, which we made into a long banner that we carried in one of the late demonstrations [fig. 17]. That's where we did the Protest Papers [cat. no. 42]. We also did the LBJ butcher aprons there.

RC: Did you live there with other artists, or was it just your place?

DD: I lived there with my wife, Judith. It was a three-story building and most of the buildings next to us were derelict or empty, so it was very quiet at night. The second floor was my studio; we lived on the top floor. We used to have film showings, underground stuff. There were other cultural things going on that were not necessarily political—it all sort of came together.

RC: When you did the LBJ aprons and the Banner, did you do them for a particular demonstration?

DD: Yeah, that was a later demonstration that we filmed. Chuck Reynolds, Tom Palazzolo, and John Heinz had 16mm cameras—some were filming in black and white but most were in color. We were documenting because we had done the banner and a bunch of LBJ aprons and were using them in the demonstration.

RC: Can you recall what was on the Banner's panels? What was the imagery?

DD: We let the artists do what they wanted. Most of it was specifically antiwar but some artists just did their own thing. As I recall we referred to the banner as "the Thing" because we carried it in a way that made it seem snakelike.

RC: Like a Chinese dragon.

DD: Right.

RC: Your loft was also the Midwest collection point for work contributed to the LA Peace Tower?

DD: Right. We crated them and we shipped them out of my house.

RC: Could you talk a bit about the Protest Papers, describe how they came up, what they were intended for?

DD: It was meant to be kind of a fundraiser, to raise money for our other antiwar activities like the Banner and exhibitions we organized outside the gallery situation. We deliberately wanted to make something stark, black and white, Posada-esque [cat. no. 42]. Very simple, nothing special aesthetically. As I recall Donley did most of the work, the silkscreening. And we invited some non-activist artists, although most of the artist community was heavily antiwar. So there was a core of us that were heavily activist and people like Richard Hunt, who was not necessarily committed [to activist causes]. Donley had it bound at the office where he worked at the time. You know, there were many people in surprising places who were sympathetic—antiwar. A lot of our propaganda—our leafleting—was printed at a place in Marina Towers run by a guy who wouldn't take any money. He would just give it to us. I went in the first time and I was flabbergasted, because I assumed he was going to give us a hard time. We didn't sell many Protest Papers. They were crude—not something you would hang on your wall. When I moved to New York we had a little money from it and we gave it to the Chicago Eight defense—maybe a couple hundred dollars.

RC: You were very active—integral to the antiwar movement, and it sounds like you were willing to take risks.

DD: I always separated my painting from political stuff; I tended not to merge the two. I was always willing to go out for demonstrations, especially in the streets because I feel that's important to move things; things don't come from the top—any change—social, political, comes from the bottom. So I tend to keep those things separate. Bob Donley and I attended a RESIST demonstration once with Benjamin Spock in Grant Park. These were people who refused to register for the draft, went AWOL, underground, or fled to Canada. And they were burning their draft cards—I remember Bob and I were out there burning things as a symbolic gesture. Dennis Kowalski also participated in a lot of these demonstrations. We got teargassed, had things thrown at us, especially during the DNC.

RC: Could you talk about making and distributing the "Landscape Beautification Johnson Style" leaflet? That remains a powerful image [fig. 18].

DD: That was totally my thing, something I had to do because all these young counterculture people were saying don't trust anyone over thirty. And yet there were more mature people out there who were active on the scene, sympathetic and turning on too. So my principal motive was to communicate to young artists that there was something else going on besides their own attitudes towards the war and the U.S. The image of the skulls came from a postcard from Guanajuato, Mexico and I made a collage with Johnson's head to imply that he was puking death. It was a parody on his wife's American "beautification" because you know she used to plant flowers along American highways and yet Johnson was destroying all these lives. I first distributed them at the student entrance at the back of the Art Institute. It was at lunch hour and I was out there distributing them to a few people trickling in. Before I knew it all these students poured out to get them. Then I started passing them out in front of the building to people coming in and out of the museum.

RC: Did you get resistance on the street from anyone; did anyone get angry at you?

DD: Not really, I didn't get much hostility.

RC: Did you or anyone in your groups have contact with DNC protest organizers like Rennie Davis, Tom Hayden or any of the Yippies who were planning to attend?

DD: We had no real contact with any of these people until the convention. During the convention we were chaperoning some of the protesters because there was a bus strike at the time and Chicago was militarized, really heavy stuff. We'd see protesters with knapsacks and we'd pick them up and bring them to Lincoln Park for instance. After clashes we'd drive the wounded who had been brutalized by the cops to churches or to Second City, which was being used as an aid station. We had contact with Abbie Hoffman but he was very suspicious of us because I was wearing a golfing jacket. It was very funny. The Yippies brought a pig that they were going to nominate for president—Pigasus for President. There was a group of them sitting in a circle doing martial arts, and they offered me a joint. We offered Abbie Hoffman a ride one night and he was very suspicious because there was a lot of undercover activity going on. In the period leading up to the convention, the police were already harassing people with their tricycles, they were running people down, women with carriages, who were just out there to see what's happening. Not necessarily radicals or anything. I remember passing a bench with two old men and an old lady and I overheard one man say to the other "why are you here?" with heavy German accents and the other man said "I'm here for the revolution." People were expecting something to happen. During the MC5 concert the cops were running their tricycles around knocking the people down. So they were instilling the violence and the fear of violence would culminate. It was mainly police violence, it wasn't demonstrators attacking police.

RC: Can you think of another instance in which you connected with a national protest effort?

DD: A week or two before the convention, I was contacted by someone from the national mobilization committee, they wanted to have an antiwar exhibit at the Coliseum in the South side, which was MOBE headquarters. So I called up the nucleus of our group and we put together a big show, good-sized paintings—we had to use work we'd already done. I met Dave Dellinger in the gallery and he thanked me for getting it together. I also remember that Irving Petlin, who as you know was heavily involved with the Peace Tower in LA, was circulating a petition to convince Picasso to remove *Guernica* from the Museum of Modern Art in protest of the war. I remember circulating that petition at the Arts Club at some opening. Richard Hunt got angry about the idea, but everyone else I approached signed it, including nonartists.

RC: Petlin was the principal designer of that famous poster that uses the text from Mike Wallace's interview with Paul Meadlo about the My Lai Massacre, "Q: And Babies? A: And Babies."

DD: Yeah, he did a lot of heavy work and still does. You know, Donley visited me in New York recently. We had breakfast and we talked about whether we had any influence, what all our activity meant.

RC: What do you think about that?

DD: Well, like I say, it was twelve years, from my first demonstration until the war ended. I pooped out at the end with the big national mobilizations when everyone had turned against the war. I figured, it's out of my hands now, it's got its own momentum. But I went to Washington a couple times after I moved to New York, not as a member of a group or as an important figure in a nucleus of any kind but just as a foot soldier. I feel like we did influence the GI movement; people at home slowly attained momentum, an organic momentum. So in that sense I feel that we had some effect because the war could have been going another twenty years if the GI's weren't revolting in Vietnam, shooting their officers. Whole platoons were refusing to fight. Officers would command a platoon to go do some action and they would say "no, fuck you, if you want it you go" so they'd call another platoon and they would say we're not going either. I guess in a sense we were partially responsible for that in a small way, like all the other antiwar groups. We had some effect but it was such a long arduous process, it was very frustrating. Twelve years: I would have never envisioned that it would have taken that long to end the war.

Dominick Di Meo was an early member of the Chicago artists' group known as the Monster Roster and works in a variety of media. He has lived in New York for many years.

Robert Cozzolino is Curator of Modern Art at the Pennsylvania Academy of the Fine Arts in Philadelphia. A specialist in American art, he has written extensively on Chicago artists.

RICHARD GRAY | *interviewed by Christopher Mack*

Christopher Mack: Tell me a little bit about what the art world was like in Chicago when you first opened your gallery.

Richard Gray: There were a small number of serious galleries, perhaps eight, in operation. I knew most of them, that's because of my own history, having been married into a collector family; although I certainly didn't think of myself as a collector at that time.

CM: The first location for your gallery was on Ontario Street, right?

RG: Yes, it was 155 East Ontario Street, the same building as Bud Holland's Gallery, but it was upstairs in a small single room. I bought an airline ticket for myself and a friend—Harry Bouras, an artist and WFMT radio commentator, who had encouraged me to open the gallery. We went to New York, where he took me around. I knew one dealer there, Noah Goldowski, a guy who used to be in Chicago and was Bud Holland's partner for many years. I decided I was devoting a certain amount of money to the gallery—I had a plan for how it was going to operate, and I bought a few things that fit into my plan and went in business. I had the first gallery opening on November 4th, 1963, so it was only two months after this first conversation with Bouras that I opened the gallery. I don't remember exactly what the show was but it consisted of the few works of art I had bought in New York by known artists. I was unknown as a dealer and I had to make an impression. I also had works of art by two or three younger artists that I got interested in, and two or three works by Gorky, De Kooning and Leger—I don't know who the other ones were.

CM: I was thinking about your operation in relation to some of the other commercial galleries of the time, and it seems to me the strategy you devised was to represent some of the "name" artists from New York, as well as some artists who worked in Chicago and may not have had the recognition that they deserved.

RG: It came out of a very quickly conceived business plan. I could tell immediately that I was going to have a very tough uphill battle, coming out of nowhere. I had never been seriously involved, I had no track record, and I had to establish an identity as quickly as I possibly could. So I thought the best way was to identify with artists people knew about and it seemed to work.

CM: So in 1966 the gallery moved from the Ontario location, right around the corner to 620 North Michigan Avenue.

RG: Yes, the gallery then moved to 620 North Michigan. After almost three years I was doing well enough to feel confident that I could move to more space. I think at about that point Phyllis Kind and her husband had opened their gallery in the same building.

CM: Could you situate the niche your gallery occupied in the late 1960s, especially in relation to some of the other major players on the scene like Richard Feigen?

RG: Richard Feigen, Bud Holland, Allan Frumkin, and Fairweather-Hardin, and Joe Faulconer's Main Street Gallery on Michigan Avenue, on the second level of his bookstore—those were the most established galleries in town. It didn't take me too long to join up with them in starting the Michigan-Ontario Gallery group, which was the precursor to the Chicago Art Dealers Association. When I went into business I had this vague idea that I would handle mainly works on paper which were affordable and had a certain appeal to me. But I soon realized that it was no way to get ahead in the art world. There was very little interest in works on paper and the pieces I had were by artists with reputations that were built around making sculpture or painting. So my focus shifted fairly quickly to a broader base including sculpture and painting and drawing.

CM: At that moment, in the mid to late 1960s, was there any sort of rivalry between artists who were active here in Chicago and those who were in New York? I know there was a lot of focus on the New York School at that point.

RG: Well there were two universes, I guess. In serious collecting much of the art world at the time was focused on artists who weren't working in Chicago, with a few notable exceptions. For the most part collectors were looking to Paris and Europe and then New York; that's what was being collected and shown by the serious dealers. The artists working locally and developing a following were the imagists including the "Hairy Who" group.

CM: So, before we get into 1968, I want to talk to you about an earlier exhibition you organized focused on works about Lyndon Johnson. Could you tell me how that show came about?

RG: First of all, my inclination, in terms of the political spectrum, was to the Left. I grew up with a proclivity for Democratic and Independent politics, although I was not very politically active. But it was a period of a lot of political unrest, and we were in the middle of a war.

CM: As I understand it, the idea for the LBJ show stemmed from the controversy surrounding Johnson's portrait that Peter Hurd was commissioned to create, which the president disliked.

RG: That's right, Peter Hurd did his portrait and the media was following it and I got this hare-brained idea that it would be interesting to do an exhibition that focused on that. We had a very short time period in which to pull this show together, just weeks. We decided to invite many of the active local artists to participate in the show.

CM: So were the works created specifically for that exhibition, or were some of the artists dealing with that theme already?

RG: They were done mainly as individual responses to the show theme; I don't know that any of them already had specific pieces made.

CM: Many of the works from the show are quick jabs at the president. Was it supposed to be a kind of flippant gesture, or did you conceive it as serious political critique?

RG: I'm certain I didn't impose any guidelines at all, except maybe for size.

CM: So you gave them the idea, and just let them run with it.

RG: It's what I would have done even now. I'm not in the habit of telling artists what to do.

CM: There were some threatening letters and phone calls during the exhibition.

RG: We got our share, which was great because it brought a lot of attention to the show. So we had a lot of traffic.

CM: And I read in one of the articles that there was a Chicago police officer stationed at the gallery during the opening. Do you remember that?

RG: That's right, I got a little panicked and I asked the local police to put someone there.

CM: So the threats were serious enough to make you concerned.

RG: Well, we were not used to that type of thing. We didn't want to take any chances, besides it added to the mystique.

CM: Richard Feigen put together a Richard J. Daley show following the Democratic National Convention and he commented later that he was trying to use the exhibition to bring some of the outrage about the violence into the mainstream, so that it couldn't be dismissed as hippie rhetoric. Did you see the 1967 LBJ show in similar terms?

RG: I think I'd have to speculate. Maybe I had partially a commercial instinct there, thinking it was something that would draw attention to the Gallery. But I think, more importantly, it was an expression of my own political orientation, which was somewhat activist at that point. I was definitely anti-war.

CM: Let's talk about the 1968 convention week. Were you in Chicago at the time?

RG: Yes; towards the middle of the week I left the gallery one afternoon to join the demonstrations and climbed the hill to where the center of the activity was in Grant Park, near the Hilton Hotel, where someone was making a speech, and I then marched with the crowd down south Michigan Avenue and ended up on the front line where the barbed wire and the jeeps were. Just north of where the jeeps were lined up was the railroad overpass. I was there, taking pictures and getting gassed. I wound up running up the street trying to get out of the gas. The next day I went up to Michigan to the old resort that was my family's business. There was a big barn I had turned into a theater. We used to have movies and chamber music and plays and all kinds of art activities. And that particular night I got up on the stage and made remarks about the convention and the demonstration. There was a huge audience, mostly from Chicago and Detroit, and people still talk to me now about that night I came back from the convention and told them what was going on. Of course it was also all over television at the same time, so everyone was aware of what was going on and extremely interested in a first-hand report.

CM: I can't even imagine what that must have been like, not only in the moment but also wondering how things would go on from that point forward.

RG: Just remembering it I get this rush of feeling right now—there was so much emotion, people were so worked up and moving in a solid, solid mass, all the way down Michigan Avenue. And all the noise and the smoke and the gas and the police and the loudspeakers whipping up the crowd. The cops were going wild because they were emotional and worked up and scared too, I am sure.

CM: A charged moment.

RG: Oh, highly charged.

CM: How would you connect that history with contemporary situations—a war with no end, a presidential administration unpopular across party lines, and another contentious election? Do you see artists today tackling political issues with the same level of frankness that some artists did in the '60s, or is it unfashionable for contemporary artists to engage in direct political statements?

RG: Whether or not its fashionable I don't know, there's no question that this generation of artists, this generation period, is not as emotionally revved up and charged as activists were then. Plenty of people are worked up about this Iraq war situation and this presidential administration, but it's nothing like it was then. It seems now that reactions and responses tend to be more measured. Artists as well as others don't seem to have the urge to be as confrontational. Just observe the present political campaign, it all seems so civilized. Where are the marches and the demonstrations, the bombastic oratory of the '60s? Have we become so complacent? Time will tell.

Richard Gray has been a distinguished dealer in Chicago and New York for forty-five years. He is a board member of the Chicago Humanities Festival, The David and Alfred Smart Museum of Art, and The Art Institute of Chicago.

Christopher Mack is Assistant Curator at the DePaul University Art Museum.

ELLEN LANYON | *interviewed by Joanna Gardner Huggett*

Joanna Gardner-Huggett: Tell me about the work you were doing around 1968.

Ellen Lanyon: By the late '60s I had turned to what you could call still life but was really based on magic and ideas about transformation and illusion. My son brought an early twentieth-century book home from school called *Magical Experiments or Science in Play*, with a lot of engravings by a Frenchman named Louis Poyet. He has become an influence through my entire body of work...even to this day I'm still harking back to Poyet as inspiration. They were illustrations for magic stunts, and also a way of teaching children chemistry and physics. A lot of the images were domestic objects; teacups and knives and forks. Then people gave me other magic books and I started getting interested in actual prestidigitation, stage productions.

Lucy Lippard came to town, and at a party we got to talking and she asked if I'd like to form a Chicago branch of WEB [West East Bag, an International Network of Women Artists, founded in 1971]. She came over to my studio and saw a big screen called "The Goddess and Reptile Illusion," and she said, "Fantastic! What a wonderful image to portray feminism." I guess I'd been doing this all along and I wasn't really thinking about that but obviously it's all there. Lucy asked if I'd like to work on WEB, and I said sure. I sent letters out to 50 women artists in the area and I invited them to a meeting. I was teaching at the School of the Art Institute so I was allowed to use space. At least 300 women showed up, everybody brought artist friends.

Marcia Tucker [a writer and critic from New York] held a meeting at Sara Canwright's loft, which was out west on Chicago or Division. Marcia talked about consciousness raising and then many groups were formed in the city. Johnnie Johnson and I participated in the WEB newsletter—sometimes 4 pages, sometimes 8 pages, typed and mimeographed and then we'd send it out four times a year for a couple of years. Then Johnnie and I organized two conferences at Oxbow [a summer artists' colony in Saugatuck, Michigan]. That's where I met Joyce Kozloff [a feminist art activist] and so many women from different places. We slept on floors, we rented a whole bunch of cots; Oxbow was very rugged in those days. From that, the first gallery started. I was exhibiting with Richard Gray Gallery and I did not participate in the formation of the galleries but I was around and connected to a lot of people.

JGH: So you were supportive of Artemisia and the ARC [Artists, Residents, Chicago], did you exhibit with them or do programming with them?

EL: I think I did, I was in a couple of theme shows but I didn't have a show there because that wasn't my place. I was already exhibiting, but I could do other things for them.

JGH: I noticed that you did a panel with Johnnie Johnson on "Economic Structures of the Art World," I think in 1973 and maybe at Artemisia as well. Was it to help women artists with practical concerns?

EL: We had several of those conferences, and I still have the transcripts from them I felt it was important for women to be able to manage their life as well as their art.

JGH: Did that happen after you were active with Lucy Lippard and with WEB?

EL: I think it must have been. A little bit after that some women started leaving home and going to New York, which I didn't do. I was at the first meeting in 1975 in New York at Joyce Kozloff's when the original Heresies [a feminist publication of art and politics 1977-92] was formed, and since I didn't live there I couldn't be part of it. But I sat at the table listening to the argument between Miriam [Shapiro], who wanted to start a school and Lucy [Lippard] who wanted to start a magazine, which we did. Then I worked on the Heresies collective.

JGH: It seems from various historical accounts that feminism came later to Chicago than New York and L.A. Do you have any thoughts about why that was the case?

EL: Chicago was a place where women were not discriminated against. Margot Hoff, Eleanor Cohen, Martyl, Lillian Florsheim, Claire Zeisler—the older generation, all of whom were my friends, we respected each other, we thought of each other as professional artists. We were never separated out; in fact we all won prizes, exhibited. I never even thought about not being a part of the art world. And I was married to an artist, and it was never a problem there, everybody did things together. I think coming around to the actual realization of what we should be about was slower.

JGH: There does seem to be a strong history of women being supported in Chicago. I know in the '30s and '40s Gertrude Abercrombie and Julia Thecla were written about.

EL: The whole Tree Studio group. I think that is the only reason I could think of. Although I had gone to New York earlier than the '60s, and then started exhibiting in 1960 with Zabriskie, I was never there for very long. I would see Miriam but she might not have even been there yet. I knew Judy Chicago later on, but not earlier.

JGH: Lucy Lippard was your first contact with the feminist art world then. How did you meet her?

EL: She came to lecture at the Art Institute; Lew Manilow, a Chicago collector, had a party, and I remember standing in the corner by a book case and this famous conversation took place. Later the women's caucus started up in the College Art Association. We all were concerned about women in the school situation...underpaid, not really given a chance for advancement. I had been hired at Cooper Union and then fired because the male teachers didn't approve of the way I was teaching—I wasn't teaching in a pedantic, draw-the-figure sort of way. There was a little jealousy there and they complained and so I was let go. When a woman became dean of the art school at Cooper she immediately hired three women, and I was one of them: one in painting, one in graphic design, and one in photography. So the caucus was a very, very, very important movement.

JGH: Did similar protests took place at other art schools (say, the Art Institute, the University of Illinois, and University of Chicago)?

EL: There was a strike at the Art Institute but it wasn't the women. Again there were a lot of women teaching there. Women were often thought of as equal to men.

JGH: At The Art Institute there was some discussion that women were not awarded fellowships in proportion to their numbers.

EL: I don't know the figures on that. It used to be that there were a lot of women in art school, because at that time it wasn't considered to be a real profession. Earlier, so many GI's came back to school, that was already 1948. So women had been in the war effort and they had learned that they could have a job and do things. People started getting married and having kids, but the art business didn't change that much, women were still privileged here anyway. I know New York was terrible. Chicago hasn't been the most active art community; they used to call it the second city or the third city. A lot of people felt there was more action in New York and moved east, and a few of them have had some notoriety, not all.

JGH: You belonged to a consciousness raising group; how many women participated?

EL: We tried to keep the groups at about eight, so it wasn't too many.

JGH: What kind of topics seemed to dominate your discussions?

EL: Mostly it had to do with people's experiences with men and—you know—compromise. By that time there were a lot of younger women who were just waking up to the idea of inequality. I'm from a generation that didn't feel discriminated against in the art world. But younger women had more of problem than I did. Certainly today it's still the same though in Chicago. There's as many women recognized as men here.

JGH: Judy Chicago wrote to you that she felt the cooperatives ARC and Artemisia were starting to overtake the work being done by WEB.

EL: They did because we just sort of faded out. Most women joined one of the co-ops; not all because they didn't have that many artists, but a lot of them did. They would exhibit and then have the chance to be in a commercial gallery and they would move on, and more women would join. Besides that WEB was really more of an organization of Miriam Shapiro and Lucy rather than Judy. At that time she and Judy were on the outs, so maybe there was a little tension there.

JGH: Let's talk a little bit more about the conferences and workshops from WEB.

EL: There were technical presentations, readings, creative writing—a perpetual round of women making presentations, either demonstrating something or lecturing on some subject.

JGH: I've also read that Harmony Hammond [an artist active in the feminist and gay liberation movements] showed a video about AIR[Artists in Residence, a women artist's cooperative found in 1972 in New York], and that this was a real catalyst for the founding of Artemisia, were you part of those conversations at that moment?

EL: Not really, but I knew most of the women and encouraged their efforts to form Artemisia. Some women rebelled against Marcia Tucker after her visit, like Lillian Florsheim and Claire Zeisler. They said "we're too old for this kind of thing. We do what we want, we don't have to join a group," and they didn't, although they should have. Both of them had a certain amount of wealth and they probably could feel more independent. Whereas I think a lot of women felt dependent on family or whatever. At the time there was a lot going on, and I just did my part of it. Johnnie then came in right after the first wave and did a lot of the work.

JGH: I've read she was very interested in teaching women to handle their finances, to learn how to pay taxes as an independent artist. I wonder how important that was because it seemed like that was part of the workshop you've done with her.

EL: Very important.

JGH: Did WEB collaborate with other feminist groups in the city—Chicago Women's Liberation Union [1969-77], their liberation school [1970-76]?

EL: Not to my knowledge. It was pretty much kept within the realm of the art world, but people belonged to other things independently.

JGH: Did you become involved in other modes of political protests in the '60s and '70s?

EL: Yes, I was a founder of Momentum and a member of the artists collective PAC and there was always something happening. I remember striking against the Hearst newspapers back in the 40s because we got bullied by deliverymen. We were active now and then with protesting racism and anti-Semitism: housing restrictions in Saugatuck, whites-only restaurants in Galena.

JGH: Were you part of the artist-led protests in 1968 with the convention?

EL: That's what we did—we had these shows. In 1968 Sally Shorey and Nora Smith, who were political activists, people of moderate wealth, and connected in the art world, started the exhibition *RESPONSE* in the fall, and Feigen did one at the same time.

JGH: Was there a split between women artists who wanted visibility and conventional success and those who had a more political and feminist agenda in the '70s?

EL: There were people like myself who said: "I am an activist, but I am not making activist art. I think through my art, I'm expressing certain things that are very much a part of the feminist movement; however, I don't do that as a protest in any way. But do you know the Joy Poe story?

JGH: I've heard about it.

EL: There was a double opening at Artemisia Gallery in 1979, in one room geometric pieces by Barbara Housekeeper and on the other very political collages by Joy Poe, who came in the afternoon of the opening and started shooting up the walls to add bullet holes, but Barbara's work also got damaged. Then at the opening itself a man came in and threw Joy to the floor and raped her; she was doing a performance but it was the real thing. People were shocked, there were children there, the whole thing was very difficult. There were other women who thought she had done a great thing. I was torn: I didn't mind so much what she had done—I thought it was very courageous because there was a lot of talk then about women being raped. But she didn't think about Barbara, and what it would mean to this other woman who was also a serious artist. That was my problem.

JGH: Did that episode have long-term effects regarding the state of art, women and feminism in Chicago?

EL: I think it made Chicago women much stronger. New York always had its bars and meeting places, and people had cliques, but there were places for people to be together. Chicago never had that. The women should have started a center where you could go and meet your friends, but there was never a place; you had to create everything.

44

Ellen Lanyon is primarily known as a painter. Her work has been shown widely in solo and group exhibitions, and she has taught in Chicago and New York.

Joanna Gardner-Huggett is Associate Professor of History of Art and Architecture at DePaul University.

ROBERT SENGSTACKE | *interviewed by Amor Kohli*

Amor Kohli: Bobby, the first question I wanted to ask you is what drew you to photography?

Robert Sengstacke: As early as I can remember I was drawing and painting and my mother always had photography books at home. I saw a copy of *The Sweet Flypaper of Life*, by Langston Hughes and Roy DeCarava, at a friend's home in 1956 and I'd go by even when she wasn't home and ask if I could look at that book: other than the Black press it was the first positive photography of African Americans that I had seen because most of the images of Blacks in the White press were going to jail or something negative. When I was 14, I got my first camera.

AK: And you'd been publishing photos in the *Defender* since you were 14, but freelancing seriously in the mid-60s?

RS: When I was 24, I had ten years of experience. I would get up in the morning and listen to John Coltrane and Eric Dolphy for two or three hours, and I'd go out with my camera and say to myself, if John Coltrane can do it with music I can do it with a camera. During that time there was a renaissance taking place in Black art in Chicago. A buddy of mine from Hyde Park High School who was a musician reconnected with me and we started checking out Black events at a time when Afros were just catching on here. I was the first one in the Black bourgeoisie to sport an Afro, the only other Blacks who wore them were musicians and a few artists, and they were getting arrested, mainly by Black cops who would say things like "what the hell are you doing with that helmet on your head?" When the cops would stop me I had a press card and as soon as I said "Sengstacke" they disappeared.

AK: Was this prior to the AACM [Association for the Advancement of Creative Musicians] being born?

RS: Yes, this was in 1964. I had shot Muhal Richard Abrams's experimental band before the AACM was formed in 1965 with all the cats who emerged from the AACM. Kalaparusha Maurice McIntyre, Anthony Braxton, Joe Jarman, Roscoe Mitchell, Lester Bowie, Malachi Favors, Thurman Barker, Christopher Gaddy, many more. There was a group of photographers around and as we got to know each other we developed a sense of responsibility to counteract negative images in the White press of African Americans. At that time there were no Black History Month celebrations or Black museums to exhibit our work; we just documented our people because we felt that in the future somebody would want to see what the Black photographer had to say about his people.

AK: So it was your way of giving back to the community?

RS: Not giving back, there was nothing to give back for, it was about love for who we were, although I had the *Defender*. That's where my work took on a sense of direction. Also, it was a period of Black consciousness because in my day the worst thing you could call somebody was black. But when Stokely introduced Black Power, all of a sudden everybody was saying "Say it loud: I'm Black and I'm proud." Things were happening— the AACM was performing at Lincoln Center and the University of Chicago, and the Afro-Arts Theater had opened.

AK: So were you one of the founding members of OBAC [Organization of Black American Culture]?

RS: Yeah, I was one of the original participants in the Visual Arts Workshop. The AACM was a collaborating organization. I remember one time Joe Jarman had a concert at Lincoln Center, now Northeastern Illinois University's Center for Inner City Studies, and I showed up unrehearsed with a slide projector and projected images from the balcony. We didn't know how it was going to be received by the audience. After the concert people said, "how did you and Joseph plan your slides with his music?" We didn't—we just put Black art with Black art and blew peoples' minds—with street scenes, stop signs, Black people doing their thing, these kinds of creative things were beginning to happen.

AK: So you were involved with OBAC, did you also get involved with COBRA [Coalition of Black Revolutionary Artists] and AfriCobra [African Commune of Bad Relevant Artists]?

RS: No, because I've never really been a joiner—partly because my father taught me that in the newspaper business, it's better to be independent. I got a t-shirt with this [points to a picture of him with Barack Obama] but that's different. I rarely wear buttons or anything like that because regardless of my personal beliefs I did not want to alienate myself from other Black movements or organizations.

AK: Was there any kind of a Black gallery scene at the time?

RS: At the time back then? No, no.

AK: Were White galleries interested in Black art?

RS: No, but both Black and White museums and universities were beginning to be. Black people weren't even that interested in Black art, although I had began collecting African art while I was still in grammar school. A few cities like Washington D.C. and New York have always been good for Black art. D.C. was really at the forefront. The boom in collecting got going in the '80s and today you have sophisticated art galleries and collectors both Black and White. When we were documenting Black people and lifestyle there was virtually nothing going on except what I mentioned. Earl Calloway and I founded the first major observance of Black History Month in the United States with "Black Aesthetics" at the Museum of Science and Industry, now known as "Black Creativity." Before that you had the Black history club here in Chicago, founded in the Wabash Y.M.C.A. by Carter G. Woodson. Then came Black history week, and we used to run stories on the Black History Club in the *Defender* but it was only one week until we extended it to two and then a month at the Museum. Black newspapers started marketing Black History Month special editions and once the White press saw there was money in it they followed suit.

AK: Was there consensus in the African American artistic community about how to present Black history—say in the Wall of Respect [a mural painted by OBAC artists in 1967 at 47th Street and Langley Avenue in South Chicago].

RS: Bill Walker was the one who proposed the Wall to the OBAC's Visual Arts Workshop. After the wall was completed, he and these two women—I don't remember their names—started a lot of dissension. The workshop had done the most positive thing in Chicago for unity that summer. Anyway, Bill Walker and Billy Abernathy were standing in front of the Wall of Respect one night—about to go to blows. All this negative shit. Walker wanted control, and and he finally got it, it broke my heart. Bill didn't like Norman Parish's work—so a few years later he painted it over it! I wasn't that crazy about the work either, to be honest with you, it was a little too abstract for me, but we would never have painted it out! Walker tried to get me to come back, I didn't want anything to do with any organization after what he had done. He apologized later, publicly. Jeff Donaldson was really angry with me for not joining AfriCobra, because not only did they want me as an artist but they wanted the Sengstacke name, they knew I was the one who kept the police off when we were doing the Original Wall of Respect, but I just didn't want to go through anything like that again, although AfriCobra never had that kind of crap and they are still together today. It was too close, too hurtful so, to some regret today, I refused AfriCobra.

AK: I wanted to ask about photography and the Wall of Respect, because when you think about public murals you don't think so much about photography as being a part of them.

RS: Yeah, but you see our pursuit was a different kind of photography because we were part of what the greatest poet of our generation Amus Mor termed the Hip Generation. We were documenting everything. The Wall of Respect became the biggest thing that summer and later the world. The neighborhood protected us. I kept the police off because Daley and the police looked at everything that Black people were doing, especially Black artists, as threatening, and police came by and attempted to intimidate the artists. As soon as I saw this I ran a photo of the Wall in progress on the front page of the *Defender* and they backed off.

AK: Were you at the dedication for the Wall of Respect? What was the mood like?

RS: Well, it was jubilant and militant. There were some police there. But there was no violence. It was too positive. Joe Jarman played music. I mean why would we build a wall just to burn it down, it wasn't about that. The little kids from the 'hood knew every figure painted on the wall, and they acted as guides for the people who came to see the wall for money, "that's Miles Davis, this is so and so, there's Malcolm X." Black consciousness was something that Black people were exploring, and that's why the Wall was so important, people would drive by in a slow line of traffic to view the Wall. The Wall was about our heroes. Malcolm X was on there—it's interesting that King was not. But see, that was the militant attitude of the times.

AK: What was the climate like for Black artists in Chicago?

RS: Mayor Daley did not want a bunch of free-thinking artists, Black or White, stretching out the minds of the city. He wanted control. He dried up the record and the film industry. Other than Haskell Wexler, who snuck off that film *Medium Cool* during the convention in '68, no movies were made in Chicago for years. Daley was even negotiating to bring Stax [Records] here from Memphis. He was so slick even Republicans stopped opposing him. He was too good for everybody, he knew how to spread the money around the neighborhoods. He had Polish folk, Lithuanian, German aldermen and then the poor Blacks on the west side and the middle class and upper-middle class Blacks on the south side. That's the way Chicago was designed politically to deal with economic and ethnic populations. Shortly before his death he was beginning to open the city back up to the arts. When I came up, as an artist Chicago was no place to be somebody. The concept about art was if you can't put it in your bank account, it ain't shit. The positive side is that Chicago and Midwest artists do well in New York because the more difficult it is to get recognition, the more creative the artists are. When Black New York wants the real fine art, it's Midwest artists that shine.

AK: You were in Miami for the Republican convention but a lot of focus here is on the '68 Democratic Convention, and what happened in Lincoln Park and Grant Park. Were you around for that?

RS: I was only in Grant Park briefly. I was assigned to cover the convention hall. I did go to Grant Park once or twice but I didn't get any of the beatings during the police riots.

AK: What were your impressions of what was going on, even in the Convention Hall?

RS: The Democrats were embarrassed; Daley wasn't going to let anybody push him around. He was not popular with my generation, especially when he issued the shoot-to-kill order during the riots. But Daley never forgot how he got there. It was my father and Congressman Dawson who put him in office through Black votes, and kept him there his first two terms. After that even the Republicans stopped opposing him. They're the reason Blacks switched over from Republican to Democrat; Dawson and my father had a deal with Franklin Roosevelt to open civil service at the U.S. Post Office to Blacks if they could get Blacks nationally to switch parties and they were successful. Today in any major city with a sizable Black population if you go into the post office, you're not going to see anything but Black faces. Go to New York, travel around Manhattan all day you might see three black police; compare that to Chicago. Look at who has had the jobs on the sanitation trucks in Chicago, in most major cities those are White jobs, because the pay is good. And you can compare how Blacks fared in Chicago to other cities with White mayors back in the day. Blacks have always fared better in Chicago. That was John Sengstacke and Congressman William L. Dawson who saw what needed to be done, did it, and kept their mouths shut. Daley was two-faced in ways but he never forgot how he came to power. Black people in Chicago don't realize there was this other side to Daley—he paid off and that's what kept him in power all those years. One time the federal government foolishly got on Daley's case about affirmative action and he said: "look, I'll match my numbers to anything you got in any federal agency." The Feds backed off and shut up.

AK: Given all that, what was the response in the community of Black artists to what had happened at the convention?

RS: By harassing and arresting so many people, the Daley administration was not popular with artists. It was part of an overall dislike of Daley and his policies and the police. But Blacks had been going through this long before 1968. We were the ones who kept the police in shape. So to us, White people were just getting a taste of what we'd had for years.

AK: Were there just more pressing issues for the Black community? Police brutality, for instance.

RS: Black people were talking about revolution. The Panthers were highly respected because they stood up. I was invited to the first organizational meeting for the Black Panthers in Chicago, in Madison Park, in a plush apartment. They were talking about printing newsletters, things that were going to cost money, and I said, "We need to figure out a way to raise some funds." "Funds? What's with all this capitalist shit you're talking?" I said, "what you are talking about costs money, that's all I'm saying." As I said before I was not a joiner—not the Panthers or anybody else, especially after the experience with OBAC. They wanted to blow up water mains and stuff. I said, "if I was going to do that I wouldn't put on a Panther uniform and mark myself, why not put on a suit and tie and go downtown and do what you are talking about, to me that makes more sense." At that point I said, "you all know Mayor Daley and he isn't going to put up with no Panthers in Chicago. You guys put on a Panther uniform, you got about a year and a half." And it was about a year and a half to the day when they murdered Fred Hampton. So I left the meeting. They didn't want to hear me, but I'm a realist.

AK: So you weren't surprised by what happened?

RS: Now Fred [Hampton] and that younger group, I don't know what they might have done but [Cook County State's Attorney Edward] Hanrahan just busted in and eliminated them. What was it, hundred bullets all going one way and not one bullet hole on the other side of the room? My cousin was shooting for the *Defender* and he went by and photographed the apartment and the blood-stained mattresses with one of Malcolm X's books on the floor.

AK: Talking about 1968, did you ever think that forty years later a Black Chicago political figure would be this close to being President?

RS: I wasn't hoping or wishing for it, but I figured eventually we're going to have everything, woman, Chinese, Mexican president someday. I don't think that when Barack Obama made that great speech at the Democratic convention that he was thinking about being president either. What I am most impressed with is how civil rights has impacted this younger generation in such a short period of time.

AK: As a photographer are you mainly concerned with producing positive images?

RS: Black people need to be spoken to in a positive way; there's too much negative shit in the world today. I have always wanted my work to have a positive universal message. I want to speak to my people in an uplifting way, but I also want to speak to all people. My work carries a universal message from a people who are looked upon as being on the bottom of society.

Robert Sengstacke is a distinguished photographer and journalist from Chicago. His family founded and published the Chicago Defender, *one of the largest and most influential African American newspapers in the country.*

Amor Kohli is Assistant Professor in African and Black Diaspora Studies at DePaul University.

Exhibition Catalogue

1.

Ralph Arnold

American, 1929–2006

Who You/Yeah Baby, 1968

Oil and collage on canvas

30 ⅛ x 24 ¼ in.

Collection of DePaul University

Art Museum,

Art Acquisition Endowment

Photograph by Tom van Eynde

3.

2.

Don Baum
American, b. 1922
L.B.J., 1967–68
Wood and glass box, head
and torso of doll, decals
10 ¾ x 8 ⅞ x 7 ½ in.
Museum of Contemporary Art,
Chicago, gift of Albert and
Muriel Newman
Photography © Museum of
Contemporary Art, Chicago

3.

Hans Breder
American, b. Germany, 1935
Homage to Chicago, 1968
Aluminum
3 x 3 x 3 ½ in.
Collection of the artist
Photograph by Tom van Eynde

4.

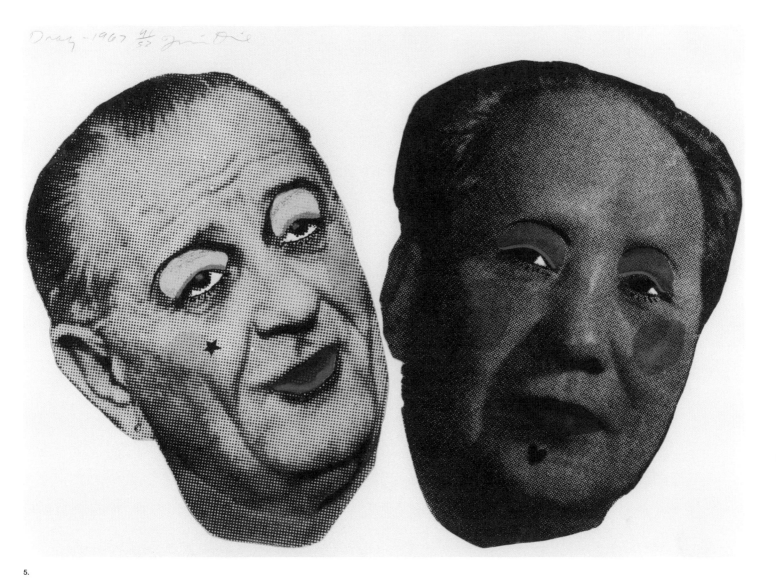

Drag -1967 4/53 Jim Dine

55

5.

4.

Dominick Di Meo
American, b. 1927
Red Queen Horizontal, 1965
Synthetic polymer and collage
on canvas
30 ¼ x 42 ⅛ in.
Collection of the artist, courtesy
Corbett vs. Dempsey Gallery
Photograph by Tom van Eynde

5.

Jim Dine
American, b. 1935
Drag: Johnson and Mao, 1967
Color photoetching
33 ¾ x 47 ¾ in.
Collection of the New School,
Art Collection, New York, NY
© Jim Dine/Artists Rights Society
(ARS), New York
Photograph by Tom van Eynde

6.

Mark di Suvero
American, b. China, 1933
Untitled (L.B. Johnson: Murderer);
from the portfolio *Artists
and Writers Protest Against
the War in Vietnam,* 1967
Lithograph on cream wove paper
21 x 26 ⅛ in.
Milwaukee Art Museum,
Gift of Mr. and Mrs. Samuel Dorsky,
M1971.34
Photography by John Glembin

LBJohnson: MURDERER

Every screaming painkick of a jelly-gasoline burnt baby

straw thatch huts Jesus! Jesus! furnaces and ovens
How many babies LBJ? How many kids did you kill today?
For love's sake For life's sake
America America become awake?
What can you do? What can you do?

This man, mad for dropping bombs
(shadow of Hiroshima when kneeling
we read in our children's eyes)
This press con-man of glib "credibility gap"
say the truth: he lies
This man who causes sons and daughters to be killed
makes war using Hitler's lie "all I Want Is Peace"
For love's sake For life's sake
America! America! become awake
what can you do?

We the people We are responsible
and the once fresh laughing baby-flesh charred into a grave
worse than a plague across this land is an accusing hand
O my people
A criminal is our head of state. Be rid of him
I impeach him now before it is too late
For love's sake For life's sake
America! America! become awake?
what can you do? What can you do?
ONLY YOU
can stop this war

($25.7 BILLION A MONTH
50,000 TONS OF BOMBS A MONTH
AVERAGE WW II ON EUROPE
43,000 TONS A MONTH

($25.7 BILLION A MONTH
50,000 TONS OF BOMBS A MONTH
AVERAGE WW II ON EUROPE
43,000 TONS A MONTH

($25.7 BILLION A MONTH
50,000 TONS OF BOMBS A MONTH
AVERAGE WW II ON EUROPE
43,000 TONS A MONTH

8.

7.

Robert Donley

American, b. 1934

Waiting, 1967

Oil on canvas

42 x 42 in.

Collection of the artist

Photograph by Tom van Eynde

8.

Ed Flood

American, 1944–85

Kick Me, 1968

Plastic and acrylic collage

11 ¼ x 11 ¼ x ¾ in.

Collection of Roy and Mary Cullen,

courtesy of Corbett vs.

Dempsey Gallery

Photograph by Tom van Eynde

10.

9.

Leon Golub

American, 1922–2004

Two Battling Nude Men,

about 1965

Chalk on vellum

39 x 24 in.

Museum of Contemporary Art,

Chicago, bequest of Ruth S. Nath

Art © Estate of Leon Golub /

Licensed by VAGA, New York NY

Photography © Museum of

Contemporary Art, Chicago

Photograph by James Prinz

10.

Red Grooms

American, b. 1937

Patriots' Parade, 1967

Lithograph on cream wove paper

22 ¾ x 33 in.

© Red Grooms / Artists Rights

Society (ARS), New York

Photograph © 2008 The David

and Alfred Smart Museum of Art,

The University of Chicago; Gift

of Dennis Adrian in memory of

Bertha Wiles

11.

12.

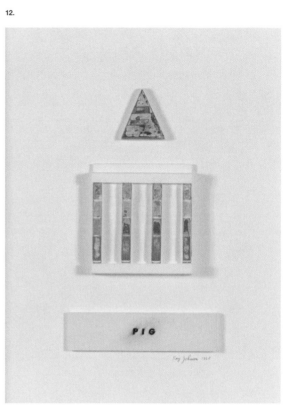

11.
Ray Johnson
American, 1927–1995
Do Not Kill, 1966
Collage on illustration board
18 ¾ x 15 ⅛ in.
The Estate of Ray Johnson at
Richard L. Feigen & Company
Photograph by Tom van Eynde

12.
Ray Johnson
American, 1927–1995
Pig, 1968
Collage on cardboard panel
17 ½ x 13 ½ in.
The Estate of Ray Johnson at
Richard L. Feigen & Company
Photograph by Tom van Eynde

13.
Ellen Lanyon
American, b. 1926
L.B.J. Doll, 1967
Pressed board, string, and pigment
35 x 21 ½ x 2 ⅜ in.
(without strings)
Collection of Betsy Rosenfield
Photograph by Tom van Eynde

14.

Roy Lichtenstein

American, 1923–1997

Pistol, 1964

Felt

82 x 49 in.

Stenn Family Collection,

Chicago, Illinois

© Estate of Roy Lichtenstein

Photograph by Tom van Eynde

15.

John Miller

American, b. 1927

Beard, 1968

Wood and leather

9¼ x 6 ¾ x 7 ⅜ in.

Collection of Roy and

Mary Cullen, courtesy of

Corbett vs. Dempsey Gallery

Photograph by Tom van Eynde

15.

16.

17.

16.
Robert Motherwell
American, 1915–1991
Iberia #18, 1958
Oil on linen
5 ⅛ x 7 ⅛ in.
Collection of the Modern Art
Museum of Fort Worth, Museum
purchase, The Friends of Art
Endowment Fund
Art © Dedalus Foundation,Inc./
Licensed by VAGA, New York NY

17.
Louise Nevelson
American, b. Ukraine, 1899–1988
Composition; from the portfolio
Artists and Writers Protest
Against the War in Vietnam, 1967
Screenprint on cream wove coated
paper
26 x 21 in.
Milwaukee Art Museum,
Gift of Mr. and Mrs. Samuel Dorsky,
M1971.32
© Estate of Louise Nevelson/
Artists Rights Society (ARS),
New York
Photography by John Glembin

18.
Barnett Newman
American, 1905–1970
Lace Curtain for Mayor Daley,
1968
Cor-ten steel, galvanized barbed
wire, and enamel paint
70 x 48 x 10 in.
Art Institute of Chicago, Gift of
Annalee Newman
© The Barnett Newman Foundation,
New York/Artists Rights Society
(ARS), New York

18.

19.
Gladys Nilsson
American, b. 1940
Snake Sleeve, 1968
Watercolor on paper
5¼ x 3¼ in.
Collection of the artist
Photograph by Tom van Eynde

20.
Claes Oldenburg
American, b. Sweden, 1929
*Proposal for a Skyscraper in the
Form of a Chicago Fireplug,* 1968
Crayon and watercolor
13 ½ x 10 ¾ in.
Whitney Museum of American Art,
New York; Gift of the American
Contemporary Art Foundation, Inc.,
Leonard A. Lauder, President
2002.50

19.

20.

22.

21.
Claes Oldenburg
American, b. Sweden, 1929
Notebook Page: Smoke Studies
During the Burning of Chicago,
1968
Spray enamel, pencil, ballpoint
pen, and collage
8 ½ x 11 in.
Whitney Museum of American Art,
New York; Gift of the American
Contemporary Art Foundation, Inc.,
Leonard A. Lauder, President
2002.53

22.
Claes Oldenburg
American, b. Sweden, 1929
Study for a Colossal Monument to
Mayor Daley #2, 1968
Crayon on paper
11 x 13 ¾ in.
Museum of Contemporary Art,
Los Angeles; Gift of Margo Leavin

23.
Claes Oldenburg
American, b. Sweden, 1929
Study of a Soft Fireplug, Inverted,
1969
Pencil
26 ¾ x 22 in.
Whitney Museum of American Art,
New York; Gift of the American
Contemporary Art Foundation, Inc.,
Leonard A. Lauder, President
2002.61

24.

Claes Oldenburg

American, b. Sweden, 1929

Three Fireplug Souvenirs—
'Chicago August 1968,' 1968

Cast plaster and acrylic

7 ½ x 7 x 6 in.

Courtesy of Richard L. Feigen & Co.

74

25.

26.
Ed Paschke
American, 1939–2004
My Pal Trigger, 1968
Oil on linen
28 x 24 in.
Collection of Daniel Cohn
Photo courtesy of the
Ed Paschke Foundation

25.
Tom Palazzolo
American, b. 1937
Campaign: The '68
Chicago Convention (still)
Film transferred to DVD
Courtesy of the artist

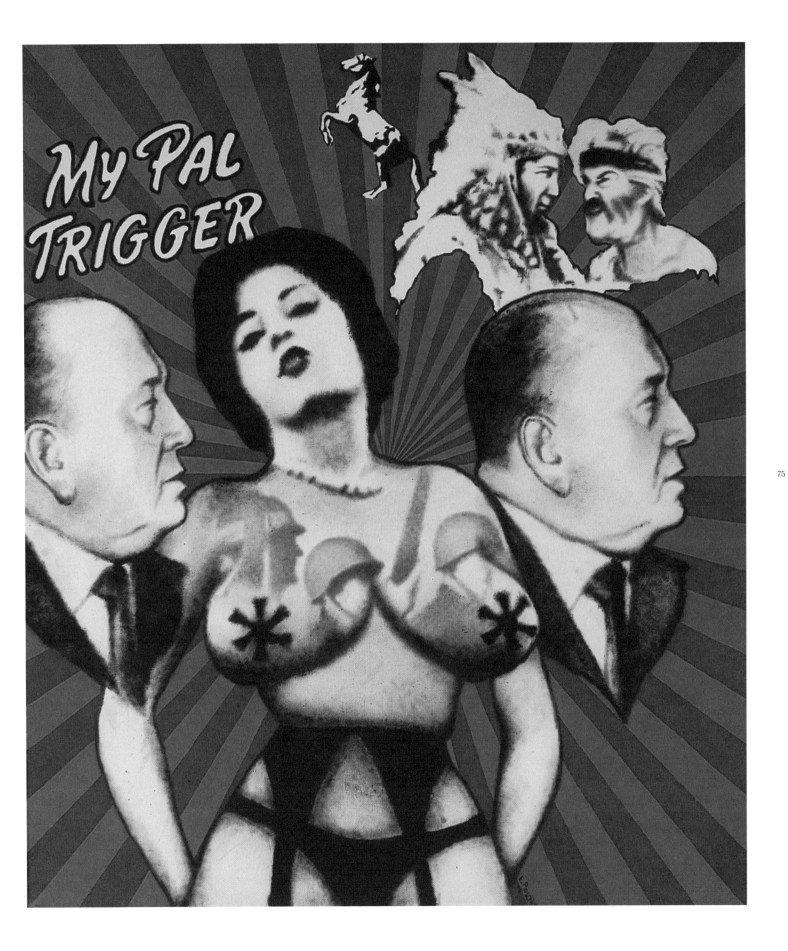

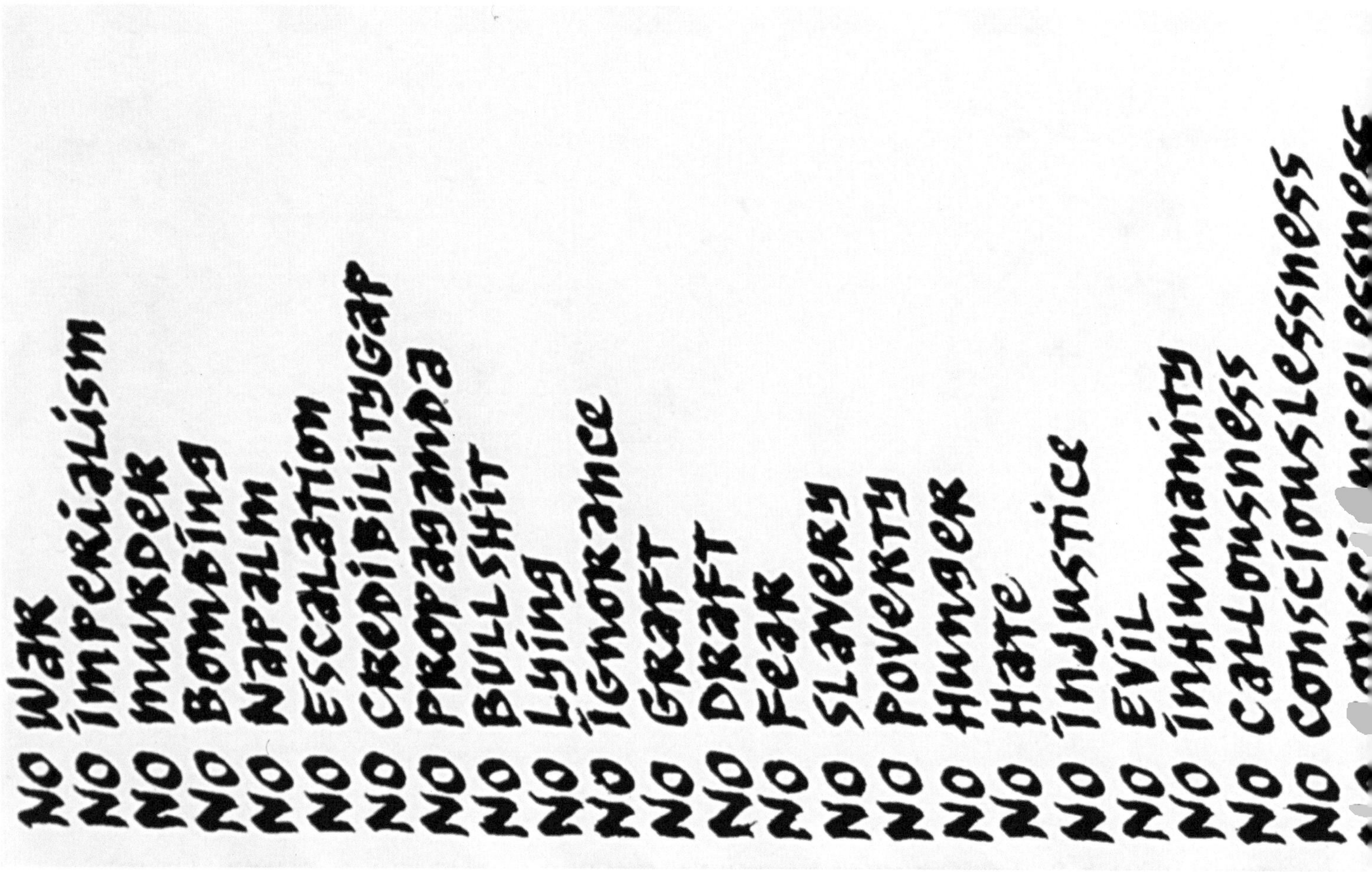

NO WAR
NO imperialism
NO murder
NO Bombing
NO Napalm
NO Escalation
NO CREDIBILITYGAP
NO Propaganda
NO BULLSHIT
NO Lying
NO ignorance
NO Graft
NO Draft
NO Fear
NO SLAVERY
NO POVERTY
NO Hunger
NO Hate
NO injustice
NO EVIL
NO inhumanity
NO callousness
NO consciouslessness
NO consciouslessness

27.

Ad Reinhardt

American, 1913–1967

Untitled (Postcard to War Chief);
from the portfolio Artists and
*Writers Protest Against the War
in Vietnam,* 1967

Color screenprint on two offset
lithographed cards, laid on ivory
wove paper

26 ⅛ x 21 in.

Milwaukee Art Museum,
gift of Mr. and Mrs. Samuel Dorsky,
M1971.31

© Estate of Ad Reinhardt/Artists
Rights Society (ARS), New York

Photography by John Glembin

NO ART OF WAR
NO ART IN WAR
NO ART TO WAR
NO ART ON WAR
NO ART BY WAR
NO ART FROM WAR
NO ART ABOUT WAR
NO ART FOR WAR
NO ART WITH WAR
NO ART AS WAR

WAR CHIEF
WASHINGTON, D.C.
U.S.A.

U.S. AIR MAIL

6c

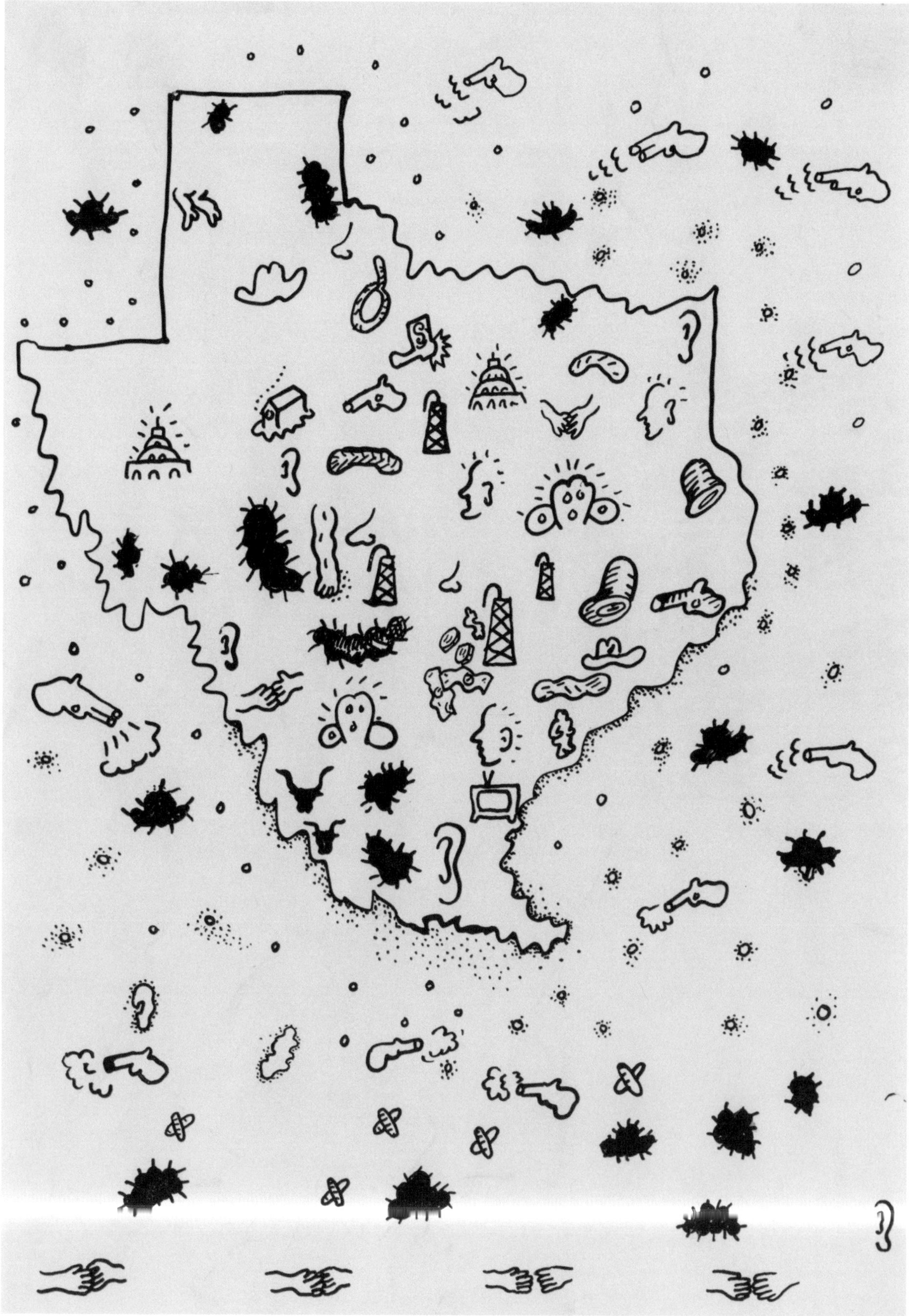

29.

28.

Suellen Rocca

American, b. 1943

The State of L.B.J., 1967

Ink on coated paper

12 ⅜ x 9 in.

Collection of Roy and Mary Cullen,

courtesy Corbett vs. Dempsey Gallery

Photograph by Tom van Eynde

29.

James Rosenquist

American, b. 1933

Mayor Daley, 1968

Oil on polyester

34 ½ x 24 ⅛ in.

Collection of the artist

Photograph courtesy

of Rosenquist Studios

80

30.

30.
James Rosenquist
See-Saw, Class Systems, 1968
Lithograph on cream wove paper
24 ⅛ x 34 ½ in.
Collection of the artist
Photograph by Tom van Eynde

31.
Seymour Rosofsky
American, 1924–1981
Daley Machine, 1968
Oil on canvas
24 x 36 in.
Estate of the artist, courtesy
of Corbett vs. Dempsey Gallery
Photograph by Tom van Eynde

32.
Peter Saul
American, b. 1934
Ching Chong (LBJ), 1968
Mixed media on board
37 x 32 in.
Collection of Susan and
Lew Manilow
Photograph courtesy
of David Nolan Gallery, New York

83

33.

33.
Carol Summers
American, b. 1925
Kill for Peace; from the portfolio
Artists and Writers Protest
Against the War in Vietnam, 1967
Color screenprint on ivory
wove cardstock
23¼ x 19 ⅛ in.
Milwaukee Art Museum,
gift of Mr. and Mrs. Samuel Dorsky,
M1971.33
Photography by John Glembin

34.
Andy Warhol
American, 1928–87
Birmingham Race Riot, 1964
Screenprint
20 x 24 in.
Collection of the Madison Museum
of Contemporary Art, Gift of the
Betty Parsons Foundation
© Andy Warhol Foundation for the
Visual Arts/Artists Rights Society
(ARS), New York

35.

William Weege
American, b. 1935
from the portfolio
Peace is Patriotic, 1967
All the Way with LBJ
Screenprints and offset litho-
graphs on cream wove paper
23 x 28 in.
Collection of the artist
Photographs by Tom van Eynde

35.

36.

William Weege
American, b. 1935
from the portfolio
Peace is Patriotic, 1967
Blessed are the Peace Makers
Screenprints and offset lithographs on cream wove paper
23 x 28 in.
Collection of the artist
Photographs by Tom van Eynde

36.

37.
William Weege
American, b. 1935
from the portfolio
Peace is Patriotic, 1967
Fuck the CIA
Screenprints and offset litho-
graphs on cream wove paper
23 x 28 in.
Collection of the artist
Photographs by Tom van Eynde

37.

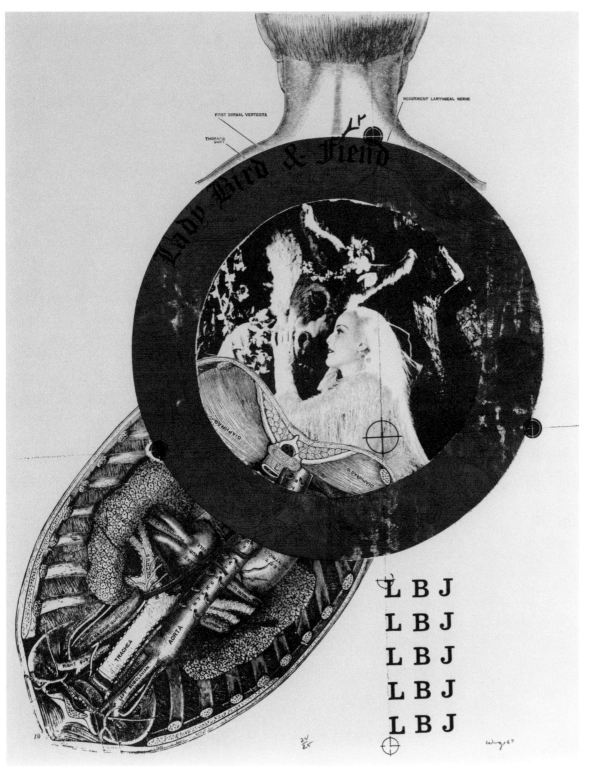

38.

William Weege
American, b. 1935
from the portfolio
Peace is Patriotic, 1967
Lady Bird and Fiend
Screenprints and offset litho-
graphs on cream wove paper
23 x 28 in.
Collection of the artist
Photographs by Tom van Eynde

38.

39.

William Weege
American, b. 1935
from the portfolio
Peace is Patriotic, 1967
My Little One
Screenprints and offset litho-
graphs on cream wove paper
23 x 28 in.
Collection of the artist
Photographs by Tom van Eynde

39.

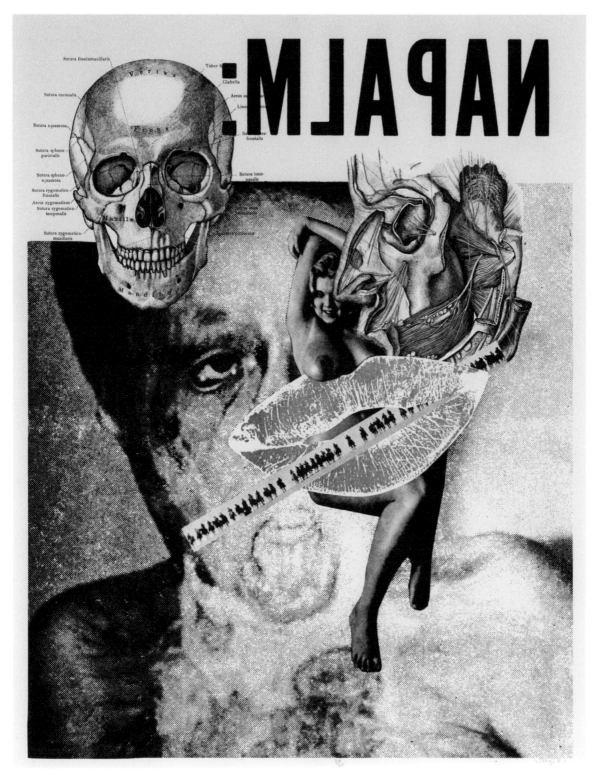

40.

William Weege
American, b. 1935
from the portfolio
Peace is Patriotic, 1967
Napalm
Screenprints and offset litho-
graphs on cream wove paper
23 x 28 in.
Collection of the artist
Photographs by Tom van Eynde

40.

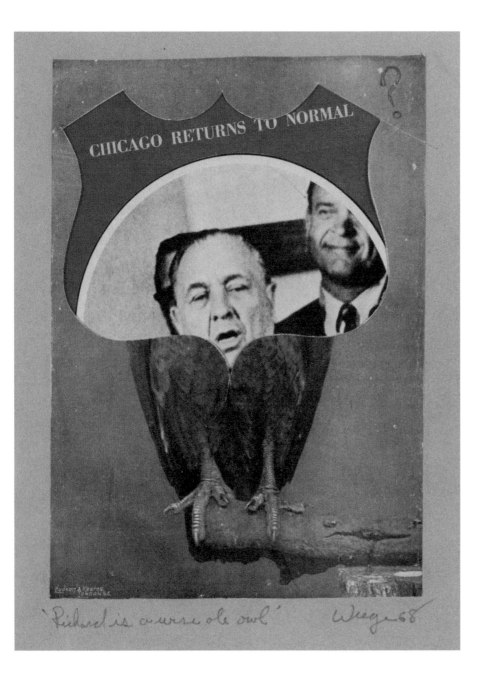

41.
William Weege
American, b. 1935
Richard is a Wise Ole Owl, 1968
Collage
14 x 10 ¼ in.
Courtesy of the Richard Gray Gallery
Photograph by Tom van Eynde

PROTEST PAPERS · VOLUME 1 · NUMBER 1

A.

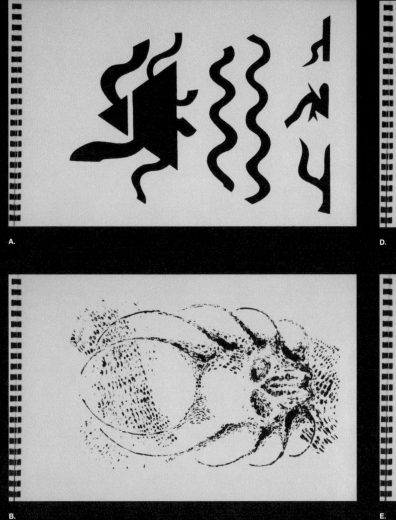

D.

94

B.

E.

C.

F.

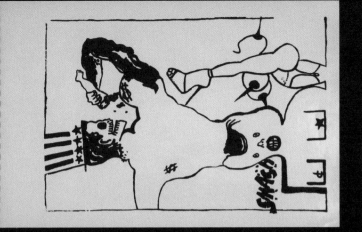

G.

J.

H.

K.

M.

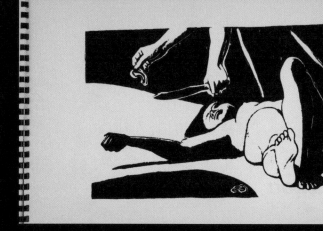

P.

N.

Q.

O.

R.

S.

T.

42.

Chicago Artists' Collaborative
Protest Papers, 1968
Screenprint (book)
Volume 1, number 1
11 x 17 in.
Collection of Corbett vs.
Dempsey Gallery

A. Jose Garcia
B. Charles B. Reynolds
C. Richard Hunt
D. Rodney Quiriconi
E. James Zanzi
F. Seymour Rosofsky
G. Mirian Brofsky
H. Eileen Schwartz
I. Vincent Arcilesi
J. Dennis Kowalski
K. Vladimir Bubalo
L. Keith Morrison
M. Allen Boutin
N. Jim Falconer
O. John McNee
P. Don Main
Q. Robert Donley
R. Thomas A. Brand
S. Jerome Walker
T. Dominick Di Meo

RS·PROTEST·P
T·PAPERS·PRO
OTEST·PAPERS
RS·PROTEST·P
T·PAPERS·PRO
OTEST·PAPERS
RS·PROTEST·P
T·PAPERS·PRO

EXHIBITION INDEX

This list is not comprehensive as it includes only artists represented in the present exhibition. Individual works shown in each historical exhibition are listed, alongside the names of additional artists who were included in the shows but are here represented by other works.

Richard Gray Gallery:
***Portraits of LBJ**, February 6— February 11, 1967*
Don Baum, *L.B.J.*, 1967/8
Dominick Di Meo
Ellen Lanyon, *L.B.J. Doll*, 1966
Gladys Nilsson
Suellen Rocca,
The State of L.B.J., 1967
Seymour Rosofsky

Chicago Coliseum,
August 27, 1968
Robert Donley, *Waiting*, 1967

Feigen Gallery: *Richard J. Daley,**
October 23—November 23, 1968
Hans Breder,
Homage to Chicago, 1968
Ed Flood, *Kick Me*, 1968
Leon Golub
Red Grooms
Ray Johnson, *Pig*, 1968
Roy Lichtenstein
Robert Motherwell, *Iberia #18*, 1958
Barnett Newman,
Lace Curtain for Mayor Daley, 1968
Claes Oldenburg,
*Three Fireplug Souvenirs—
'Chicago August 1968,'* 1968
Claes Oldenburg,
*Study for a Colossal Monument
to Mayor Daley #2*, 1968
James Rosenquist, *Mayor Daley
and See-Saw*, Class Systems, 1968
Seymour Rosofsky,
Daley Machine, 1968

Richard Gray Gallery:
***William Weege** (part of **Response**,
see p. 26), November 1968*
William Weege,
Richard is a Wise Ole Owl, 1968

Philip Freed Gallery of Fine Art:
***Portfolio–Artists' and Writers'
Protest** (part of **Response**),
November 1968**
Mark di Suvero, *Untitled
(L.B. Johnson: Murderer)*, 1967
Louise Nevelson,
Composition, 1967
Ad Reinhardt, *Untitled
(Postcard to War Chief)*, 1967
Carol Summers, *Kill for Peace*, 1967

**Allan Frumkin Gallery
(part of *Response*),
November 1968**
Tom Palazzolo, *Campaign:
The '68 Chicago Convention*

**Special Chicago Artists'
Show–Response
(part of *Response*),
November 1968**
Ralph Arnold
Don Baum
Dominick Di Meo
Robert Donley
Ed Flood
Ellen Lanyon
John Miller, *Beards*, 1968
(artist was represented,
actual work likely included)
Ed Paschke, *My Pal Trigger*, 1968
Seymour Rosofsky

**Museum of Contemporary Art,
Chicago: *Violence in Recent
American Art*, November 8, 1968—
January 12, 1969**
Ralph Arnold
Dominick Di Meo
Jim Dine,
Drag: Johnson and Mao, 1967
Ed Flood
Ray Johnson, *Do Not Kill*, 1966
Ellen Lanyon, *L.B.J. Doll*, 1966
Roy Lichtenstein, *Pistol*, 1964
Ed Paschke
Peter Saul
Carol Summers,
Kill for Peace, 1967
Andy Warhol,
Birmingham Race Riot, 1964

William Weege, *Fuck the CIA* from
the portfolio *Peace is Patriotic*, 1967

**Feigen Gallery, *Claes Oldenburg:
Constructions, Models, and
Drawings, April 30–May 31, 1969***
Claes Oldenburg,
*Proposal for a Skyscraper in the
Form of a Chicago Fireplug*, 1968
Claes Oldenburg, *Notebook Page:
Smoke Studies During the Burning
of Chicago*, 1968
Claes Oldenburg, *Study of a Soft
Fireplug, Inverted*, 1969

This catalogue was
designed at Froeter
Design Company,
Chicago. The text
face is Helvetica
Neue and Century
725 BT. The printing
of this catalogue was
completed with Ace
Graphics, Naperville.

Museum staff:
Louise Lincoln,
Director

Laura Fatemi,
Assistant Director

Christopher Mack,
Assistant Curator

Dominick Fortunato,
Intern